One Stormy Day

Sugar Creek Gang

One Stormy Day

by
Paul Hutchens

MOODY PRESS
CHICAGO

Copyright 1946 by
PAUL HUTCHENS

All rights reserved.

Moody Press Edition 1985

9 10

1

THE TROUBLE the Sugar Creek Gang had with our new teacher started the very first day we started to school again after our Christmas vacation. As you maybe know, we all had gone down to Cuba by airplane and had just come back and found that while we were gone our pretty lady teacher had gotten married and had resigned from being teacher and we were going to have a *man* teacher instead, to finish out the year—imagine that! A *man* teacher for the Sugar Creek school, when all we'd ever had, had been *lady* teachers whom we'd all liked. We were all plenty mad— *plenty!*

We might not have had all the trouble though, if it hadn't been for Shorty Long, the new tough guy who had moved into our neighborhood and who was just starting to our school.

As I said, the trouble started the very first day we started again . . . Just before eight o'clock that morning I was flying around in our house like a chicken with its head off, looking for my cap and mittens and asking Mom if my lunch box

5

was ready, and Mom was trying to keep Charlotte Ann, my baby sister, quiet so Mom and I could hear; Pop was in the living room trying to listen to the morning news on the radio, and Poetry, the barrel-shaped member of our gang, was out by the big walnut tree near our front gate whistling and yelling for me to hurry up or we'd be late, and I couldn't find my arithmetic book—which are all the reasons why, that morning, I wasn't in a very good humor to start off to school. So it was the easiest thing in the world for me to get mad quick, when, about ten or maybe fifteen minutes later, we met Shorty Long, the new tough guy who'd moved into our neighborhood, down at the end of the lane . . .

Pretty soon though, I was out of our house, slamming the door after me and dashing out through the snow path I'd shoveled that morning myself, toward Poetry, who as I said, was at the gate, waiting.

I wasn't any further than twenty noisy steps away from the house when I heard the kitchen door open behind me, and my Pop's big voice thundered out after me, and said, *"Jasper!"* which is my middle name, and which I don't like. My whole name is William Jasper Collins, but I'd rather be called just plain "Bill," 'cause that is what the gang calls me, and besides Pop never called me Jasper except when I had done something wrong or he thought I had. So when my

6

Pop thundered after me, "JASPER!" I stopped dead in my tracks, and looked back, and say! Pop's big bushy, reddish blackish eyebrows were down, and his jaw was hard-looking and I knew right away I'd done something wrong.

"What?" I called back to him, starting to go toward the gate again. "I've got to hurry or I'll be late."

"Come back and shut the door *decently!*" Pop said, and when Pop says things like that to me like that, I nearly always obey him *quick,* or wish I had.

I was half way back to the door when Poetry's squawky voice squawked to me from the gate, saying "Hurry up, Bill!" which I did. I dashed back to our kitchen door and started to shut it decently, when Pop stopped me and said, "Remember now, son, you boys behave yourselves today. Mr. Black is a fine man and you'll like him all right just as soon as you get used to him!"

"We *won't,*" I said, thinking how I'd already made up my mind I *wasn't* going to like him, 'cause he was a *man* teacher, and 'cause we'd never had a man in the Sugar Creek school, and also 'cause we had all liked our pretty lady other teacher so well, we didn't want anybody else!

"What do you mean—you *won't?*" Pop said, still holding the door open so I couldn't shut it decently. "You mean you won't behave yourselves?"

7

"I'll be *late!*" I said to Pop. "I've got to go—Poetry's *waiting* for me!"

Say, my Pop raised his voice all of a sudden and yelled to Poetry, "Hold your horses, Leslie Thompson," (which is Poetry's real name), "the first bell hasn't rung yet!" And it hadn't. When it *would* ring, there would still be a half hour for us to get to school, which didn't start until half past eight. But we all liked to get there early, so we could see each other again, none of us having seen all of us for two or three days. We might meet some of the gang on the way—Circus, our acrobat, Big Jim, our leader, Little Jim, the grandest Christian in the gang, and Dragonfly, the pop-eyed member of the gang, and maybe Little Tom Till, the new member of the gang whose big brother, Bob Till, had caused us so much trouble last year but who had quit school and had gone away to a city and was working in a factory.

You know, about every year we had some new boy move into our neighborhood, and nearly always we had trouble with him, until he found out whether he was going to get to run the gang or just going to *try* to, and always it turned out that he only *tried* to. We always had to decide also whether the new guy was going to be a *member* of the gang—and sometimes he couldn't be.

"Jasper Collins!" my Pop said to me, still holding our back door open so I couldn't shut it decently, and also holding onto my collar with

8

his other hand, "you're not going another inch until you promise me you'll treat Mr. Black decently . . . *Promise* me that!"

Just that second my Mom's voice called from some part of our house and said, "For land's sake, shut the door! We can't heat up the whole farm!"

"I *can't!*" I yelled back to Mom. "Pop won't let me!"

Well, that certainly didn't make my Pop feel very good to have me say that, and I shouldn't have said it, 'cause it was being sarcastic or something. Anyway, Pop tightened his grip on my collar and kinda jerked me back and said to me under his breath so Poetry wouldn't hear it, "We'll settle this tonight when you get home—in the woodshed—and be sure to come home early!"

I looked at our red-painted woodshed where I'd had maybe six or seven lickings from my Pop the year before, and I had made up my mind that there wouldn't be so many in the new year.

"Can I go now, then?" I said, and Pop said, "Yes"— still under his breath—"I can't very well correct you while Poetry is here"—which is one reason why I liked my parents—they never gave me a hard calling down or a licking when we had company, but always waited till later.

Say, the very second my Pop let me loose I shot away from our back door like a rock shooting out of a boy's sling, straight for Poetry and our front gate . . . I got to where Poetry was holding the gate open for me, just as I heard my Pop shut our back door decently, and Poetry and I were already talking and listening to each other and being terribly glad to be together again, when our kitchen door opened again and my Pop's big voice thundered after me, "BILL!"

"What?" I yelled back at him, and he yelled back to me, "Shut that *gate*," which I ran back and did without saying anything. A jiffy later Poetry and I were swishing through the snow toward Sugar Creek school—not knowing it was going to be the beginning of a very exciting day and also the beginning of a lot of new trouble for the Sugar Creek Gang . . .

We were ker-squashing along through the snow, making our own snow path with our feet, there not having been any cars or sleighs on our road yet that morning 'cause ours wasn't an arterial road, and Poetry said all of a sudden, "My Pop says we've got to like the new teacher."

"My Pop told me the same thing," I said, and sighed, and knew it was going to be hard to like somebody I already didn't like . . .

Well, in a few jiffies we came to the north road, where we saw, coming across the Sugar Creek bridge, two boys and a lot of girls. Right away I knew the girls were Circus's sisters, one of them being named Lucille, and was maybe the nicest girl in all the Sugar Creek school and was just my age, and she wasn't afraid of spiders and mice and things, and sometimes she smiled at me across the schoolroom . . . And say, walking right beside Lucille on the other side of Circus was another guy, and it was Shorty Long, the new boy who'd moved into our neighborhood, and whom I didn't like.

"Look!" Poetry said to me, "Shorty Long is carrying two dinner pails!"

"He's fat enough to *need* two," I said, and didn't like him even worse.

"Looks like it's Lucille's pail," Poetry said, and the very minute he said it I knew what he meant . . .

Almost right away I wondered if there was maybe going to be another fight between me and Shorty Long . . . I had a fierce one just before Christmas and just before the Sugar Creek Gang had flown down to Cuba.

Just that minute I heard Shorty Long raise his voice and yell to us something in that crazy new language he'd started us all to talking and which Dragonfly liked so well, and which is called Openglopish—which you talk by just putting an "op" in front of all the vowel sounds in your words . . . And this is what Shorty Long yelled to us:

"Hopi, Bopill! Hopi, Popo-opetropy!"—which is Openglopish for "Hi, Bill! Hi, Poetry!"

I really think I would have liked the language if Shorty Long hadn't been the one to start it in the Sugar Creek neighborhood . . .

Before I knew what I was going to say, I said,

11

looking at Lucille's red dinner pail in Shorty Long's fat left hand, "Keep still. Talk English! Don't call me 'Bopill!' Take that other syllable off!''

Even as far away as I was I thought I saw his red face turn redder, and then he yelled to me and said, "All right, if you don't want to be a good sport . . . I'll take it off . . . From now on you're just plain *'Pill—Pill* as in *catapillar.'* ''

And that started the fuse on my fiery temper to burning very fast . . . I saw red right away, and Lucille's red dinner pail didn't help any . . . Besides I was already mad from having all that trouble with my Pop . . . Besides, also I'd always carried Lucille's dinner pail myself once in awhile, when Big Jim was along and he carried our new minister's daughter's pail at the same time . . .

In fact, it was Big Jim's being especially polite to Sylvia, our new minister's daughter, which got me started being kind to a girl myself—girls belonging to the human race, also.

"I'll carry your pail for you," I said to Circus's sister, and started to reach for it, but Shorty Long interrupted my hand and said loftily, "Don't disturb the lady!" He swung his whole fat body around quick and shoved me terribly hard with his shoulder and walked on beside Lucille. At the same minute, my boots got tangled up in each other and I found myself going down a deep side-ditch backward and sideways and headfirst all at the same time into a big snowdrift—which was the beginning of the fight.

Just as I was trying to untangle myself from myself and struggle to my feet, I heard a couple of yells coming from different directions and I looked up just in time to see Little Jim and Dragonfly coming running from across the woods . . . And at the same time, I heard a fierce little girl's voice saying, "*Smarty!* You can't *carry* my pail! I'll carry it myself!"

I looked up from my snowdrift just in time to see Shorty Long whirl around with the red dinner pail in his fat left hand and hold it out so Circus's sister couldn't reach it, and also just in time to see a pair of flying feet which looked like Dragonfly's, make a dive for Shorty Long, and right away there were three of us in that big snowdrift at the same time . . . Also at the same time, I heard a dinner pail go squash with the sound of a glass and maybe a spoon or a fork or something in the pail and that was that . . .

Well, all I had to do was to swish over on my stomach and I was on top of Shorty Long; and being mad, I felt as strong as the village blacksmith whose "muscles on his brawny arms were strong as iron bands." So I yelled and grunted to Shorty Long between the short pants of my breath, "You *will* forget to wash your face in the morning, will you! Doesn't your mother teach you to wash your dirty face when you get up in the morning and before you to to school? *Shame* on you!'' . . . All of a sudden remembering I'd forgotten to wash mine. Right away I was scooping up handfuls of snow and washing Shorty's Long's face and neck, and saying to him, ''I'll teach you to throw an innocent girl's dinner pail around like that!''

Boy, oh boy, I tell you, I felt fine, on top of Shorty Long and imagining how everybody up in the road was watching me and feeling proud of me—even Circus's sister would be proud of me, a *little* guy licking the stuffin's out of a great big lummox like Shorty Long! Why, I wasn't even hardly half as big as he was, and I was licking him in a fight right in front of everybody! I tell you it felt good!

Just that minute I heard the school bell ring, and I knew we all ought to get going if we wanted to get to school ahead of time and sort of look at the teacher, and maybe I ought to clean out my desk a little, too, not having done it the last day before our Christmas vacation had begun . . .

So, I jerked myself loose from Shorty Long, scrambled to my feet, shook my cap and knocked off some of the snow, and climbed back up into the road again, where I thought everybody was who had been watching the fight . . . I guess

14

maybe I really expected them to say something about the wonderful fight I'd won, but would you believe it? . . . the girls and Poetry had walked on up the road . . . I looked around for the red dinner pail, and also for mine . . . But the red one wasn't anywhere around. Then I saw it swinging back and forth in Circus's sister's hand, about fifty feet up the road.

"I'll carry it for you," I said when I caught up with the rest of the crowd, and would you believe *that* . . . It was the most disgusting thing that ever happened, and it made me mad all over the inside of me . . . That awkward girl I'd made a fool out of myself to be a hero for, didn't even appreciate all I'd done, not even the fact that I'd given some of my life's blood for her, which I had, for my nose was bleeding a little; and for the first time I noticed my jaw hurt too, where Shorty Long must have hit me and I hadn't felt it before . . .

She kinda looked at me like I was so much chaff blowing out of a threshing machine and said, "Can't you live one day without getting into a fight? I think Shorty Long is nice."

Well, that spoiled my day, in fact it looked like it had spoiled my whole life maybe . . .

"All right, Smarty," I said, "you can work your own arithmetic problems this year." . . . And I walked behind them and on the other side of the road all the rest of the way to our red brick schoolhouse, which with its two front windows and its one door between them, and the little roofless porch, looked kinda like a red-faced boy's face, with a scowl on it . . .

" 'Smatter?" I heard somebody say beside me, and it was Little Jim, swishing along, carrying his stick in one hand and his dinner pail in the other . . .

"Nothing," I said, but felt better right away. Little Jim could do that to a guy—make him feel better, just by asking, "Smatter?" which he always did when I was bothered about something.

"Pop says we have to *like* Mr. Black, the new teacher," Little Jim said, and struck real hard at a chokecherry shrub that was growing close to the road, knocking snow off of it, some of the cold snow hitting me in the hot face and feeling good.

I didn't say anything. Little Jim's mentioning his Pop made me think of mine, and I remembered that he'd said, "We'll settle it tonight in the woodshed," so I kept on walking along, not saying anything else—not even wanting to say anything else, but knowing my whole day was ruined.

The very next thing Little Jim said didn't help me feel any better either, when he said, "We found out last night that Shorty Long's first name is 'William.' "

Little Jim struck at another chokecherry shrub which scattered some more snow in my face, and

16

I said, "WHAT! Why—that's *my* first name! How'd you find out? Who told you?"

"*His* Mom told *my* Mom," Little Jim said. "She went to church with us last night, you know."

I'd seen Mrs. Long's sad face last night while she sat in our little church with the Foote family— Little Jim's last name being *Foote*. As you know Little Jim's Mom is the pianist in our church and is maybe the best player in all Sugar Creek territory. Also Little Jim's parents are always looking for somebody to take to church and are what my Pop calls "soul winners"—that is, they are always trying to get somebody to become Christians.

"Mom wants to get Shorty Long's Mom saved," Little Jim said. He was socking every chokecherry shrub we came to, and I was getting madder and madder at Shorty Long for spoiling my whole day, also I was holding onto my nose tight with my handkerchief to help it stop bleeding.

"Is Shorty Long's *Pop* saved?" I asked.

Little Jim socked a tall snow-covered mullein stalk with his stick, knocking off the snow and some brown seeds at the same time, and what he said at the time came out of his small mouth like he had *thrown* his words at me very hard, "Nope! . . . And he's mad at some of the Sugar Creek Gang for being mean to his boy. He's told our new teacher we're a gang of rough-necks and to look out for us!"

17

"Did Shorty Long's Mom tell your Mom that?"
I asked.

Little Jim said, "Yep, last night in our car—"

Then Little Jim stopped with his stick in the air, and looked over and up at me and kinda whispered, "Shorty Long won't go to church 'cause his Pop won't . . . Maybe his parents'll get a divorce, Mom said, if they don't get saved first."

"A divorce?" I said. "What for?"

" 'Cause William's Pop is too mean, and swears so much at his Mom, and doesn't want her to go to church."

I could hear Dragonfly and Shorty Long behind me talking like they were good friends—and would you believe it? They were talking that crazy Openglopish language, just chattering back and forth like they were the very best of friends.

"But they don't call him *Bill*," Little Jim said, still talking about Shorty Long's first name. "They call him *William*."

All the time Dragonfly and Shorty Long were getting closer and closer behind us, and I could hear their crazy words which they were tossing back and forth to each other like two boys throwing soft balls back and forth to each other. Just that minute Shorty Long said, in Openglopish, "Mopistoper Blopack opis swopell. OpI'll bopet hope gopives Bopill Copollopins opa lopic-kopin' topodopay . . ." And I knew exactly what he had said and it was, "Mr. Black is swell. I'll bet he gives Bill Collins a lickin' today."

I pressed my lips together tight, and kept still, making up my mind at the same time I *wasn't* going to get any licking. We all hurried on toward the schoolhouse. The minute I got there I went straight to the iron pump near the big maple tree and put some cold water on my face and nose, washing off some of the good red blood I'd shed for a worthless girl, the cold water helping to make my nose stop bleeding. I also rinsed out my handkerchief, being especially glad my Mom had made me take two with me, which she nearly always does in the wintertime just in case I catch a cold or something, which I sometimes do.

While I was washing my face, Poetry came over and watched me, and said, "You certainly licked the stuffin's out of William Long."

"Thanks," I said . . . "But what'd they ever give him that crazy name for?"

And before the day was over, I wished even my name hadn't been William either—in fact, even before the morning had hardly got started, I was into trouble with Mr. Black—and it all happened on account of Shorty Long and I having the same first name . . . I even hate to tell you what happened, but it's all a part of the story, so here goes . . .

First thing, though, before school took up, we all got together in the school woodshed and held a special gang meeting. I told the gang what Little Jim told me that his Mom said Shorty Long's Mom said about what Shorty Long's mean Pop told Mr. Black about the Sugar Creek Gang being a bunch of rough-necks.

Then we all voted that we wouldn't *be* that. We were going to prove to our new teacher that we *weren't*.

Just before the last bell rang, Big Jim gave us all orders to behave ourselves, and said, ''If any of us doesn't behave, he'll have to be called in and stand trial by the rest of us.''

Then the bell rang, and in we went.

2

IT'S A CRAZY feeling, coming back to school after a swell Christmas vacation, and having to have a new teacher, a *man* teacher with shell-rimmed glasses and a head that is bald in the middle, and maybe forty years old, and who has one all-gold tooth right on front. Seeing that one all-gold tooth made me think of Dragonfly whose large front teeth were much too large for his very small face. I looked across the schoolroom from where I was sitting, to Dragonfly who was next to the wall beside the front window, and he happened to be looking at me at the same time. School had been going on for a long time and it was maybe after eleven o'clock, and the first grade was up on the long bench in front of Mr. Black's desk, with different ones in the first grade standing whenever Mr. Black told them to, and coming to stand beside him where he sat at his big desk, and reading out loud, making it hard for the rest of us to study, which it always is in a one-room school anyway.

Dragonfly had a mischievous grin on his always mischievous face and just as I looked he folded a little piece of paper, which he'd been writing on, slipped it across the aisle to Poetry, who slipped it across another aisle to Circus, who slipped it across to me . . . Mr. Black was very busy and I had already made up my mind that because the lenses of his glasses were very thick, he probably couldn't see back in the schoolroom very far, but could see better while he was reading, if his glasses were on.

I was supposed to be studying geography at the time, and I had my great big geography book standing up on my desk in front of me. It was the easiest thing in the world for me to unfold the note Dragonfly had sent across to me, and read it without Mr. Black seeing me do it, and this is what I read in Dragonfly's crazy handwriting: "Some people have their hair parted on the left side, some have it parted on the right, others have it parted in the middle, and still others have it DE-parted in the middle."

Well, it was an old joke which I'd heard before, but it was the funniest thing I had thought of for a long time and because I had been sad or mad nearly all morning, when I read that crazy note in Dragonfly's crazy handwriting, I couldn't help but snicker out loud, which I did. But say, Mr. Black was not only able to see all over that one-room schoolroom, but he was able to *hear* all over it, too. And so also was I.

All of a sudden he jerked up his bald head and looked right straight toward me and said, "Young man! You may stay in after school tonight!" which didn't sound very good on account of my Pop had wanted me to come home early for some reason.

"ALSO," Mr. Black said,—and his voice was a little kinder than it had been—"you may lay your book down flat on the desk!" Then he let the little girl, which was one of Circus's smaller sisters, whose name was Elfinita, sit down on the front seat of the recitation bench beside another little girl whose name was Suzanna. Then Mr. Black pushed back his big swivel chair, stood up, looked out over the schoolroom, cleared his throat and said to all of us, and maybe to me in particular, "Students of the Sugar Creek School, there is only one rule for you to obey. I will write that rule on the blackboard."

He whirled around like he meant business, looked for and found an eraser, swished it across some arithmetic problems that were there, and taking a piece of chalk, wrote the rule in great big letters, which could be seen from every corner of the room, "Behave Yourselves!" Then he laid the chalk down, sat down in his noisy chair, and went on with his class.

But almost every two or three minutes, it seemed, he would look in my direction and I knew that I had started off on the wrong foot—in fact, it was Dragonfly's wrong foot I'd started off on. I was wondering if Shorty Long's Pop had not only told Mr. Black we were a bunch of rough-necks, but that maybe I was the worst one.

I tucked the note into my pocket the very first minute I had a chance, making up my mind that the first chance I had I'd tear it into a thousand pieces and toss it into the big, round Poetry-shaped stove in the center of the room, which was going full blast that morning, making the schoolroom almost too hot for all of us.

But the real trouble came when it was time for my arithmetic class to recite. Mr. Black called us to come to the recitation bench in front of his desk, and all of the boys who were in that class got up out of our seats and went forward and sat down, there not being any girls in the class. I noticed that Shorty Long was not in the same class I was, and I was glad of it.

Well, I was still feeling pretty bad and pretty mad, and also trying not to remember the note Dragonfly had sent to me, and which was still in my pocket—you know, that note about some men's hair being parted on the left side, some parted on the right, other men's hair being parted in the middle, and still others having it DE-parted in the middle. There were just three of us in that arithmetic class—Poetry, Circus and me . . .

Maybe I ought to tell you that the very first thing Mr. Black did when school had started that morning was to have each one of us write his name on a blank sheet of paper and hand it in to him. I could tell that he had a good memory and that he would be able to remember who all of us were, most school teachers being very smart. I guess I didn't realize that I was only half sitting down, that I was almost *lying* on my back on the front bench, I was slid down so far, with my feet sticking out in front of me with the heels resting on the edge of the platform. In fact, I had one of my shoes on top of the other one, thinking about how long my feet looked, and Poetry who was sitting beside me had his feet the same way, each one of us knowing that the teacher couldn't see our feet because he was on the other side of the desk, Poetry having the biggest feet of any of the Sugar Creek Gang, as you maybe know.

Well, the top of Poetry's top foot was almost three inches higher than the top of mine was, but we were being very careful not to touch the back of the desk because that would scratch it and also because the teacher might hear our feet and know what we were doing.

All of a sudden Mr. Black's big voice said, "Long, sit up!"

In my mind's eye I could see Shorty Long, whose seat was right behind the recitation bench, all slumped in his seat and I felt good inside that he was getting called down. I guess right that minute I didn't realize that I was all slid down like I was, 'cause I had been thinking about how long Poetry's and my feet were, and it being an arithmetic class, I was dividing the three inches which Poetry's feet were longer than mine, by two, and was thinking that each one of his feet was one and one-half inches *longer* than mine.

Mr. Black looked like he was looking right straight at me through those thick-lensed glasses, and he said again, "LONG! I said SIT UP!"

Well, there was a shuffling noise behind me, and in my mind's eye I could see Shorty Long sitting up as straight as his fat body could. All of us sat real still, when all of a sudden, Mr. Black pushed back his big chair, stood to his feet, swished around the corner of the desk over to where I was, stepped down off the platform, glared down at me and almost shouted, "When I tell you to sit up, I mean SIT UP!"

And Wham! Whack! WHAM! . . . just like that I got my ears boxed hard three times.

Well, one of my jaws was already sore from the sock Shorty Long had given me on the way to school, but I couldn't believe my ears, I was so stunned.

I spoke up quick and said, "Mr.—Mr.—" and then I jerked myself up into a straight position and said, "Honest, Mr. Black, I didn't know you were talking to *me!* I thought you were talking to Shorty Long!"

Say, he glared down at me and said, "Isn't your name *William?*"

"Ah—yes," I said, "my name's William, but not W—William *Long;* my name's William COLLINS!"

And then it dawned on me what had happened. When we had handed in our names that morning on a blank piece of paper, Shorty Long had written his name down as William *Long* and I had written mine as William *Collins,* and Mr. Black had got our names mixed up, and that's how I happened to get my ears boxed.

Say, he just stood there and looked down at me and kept on looking, and all the time I was feeling worse 'cause things were all so mixed up. I guess he was still angry too, anyway he didn't seem to be sorry he had made such a terrible mistake, 'cause he said, "You can take that punishment for snickering out loud in school, then . . . Besides, the recitation bench is *not* a place for a mid-morning nap!"

"Ye-yes, sir," I said, as politely as I could. I was trying to remember something my Pop had told me, quoting from the Bible, and it goes something like this, "Angry words stir up wrath!" which means if you say angry words to people, it'll make *them* mad too . . . Also, if you say angry words to people, it helps to make you still madder yourself . . . And the way to cool off after a fight is to start using kind words instead of mad ones. The fierce look in Mr. Black's eyes made me realize I ought to start making up with him right away.

He was still glaring at me, then all of a sudden he folded his arms and stared straight through me, and said, "William Collins, you may hand me that note in your pocket!"

Well, that was too much. All of a sudden, in my mind's eye I could see the whole world falling upside down not only for me but for the rest of us, but I remembered about using kind and respectable words, so I said, politely, "What note, Sir?"

"The one in your pocket—I was going to wait until after school for it, but I'll take it *now* . . .Since it was passed during school hours and since so many boys had a share in passing it on to you—"

Say, all of a sudden, Big Jim spoke up from the back of the room and said, "Mr. Black, may I say a word?"

Mr. Black raised his eyes and looked back to the back of the room where Big Jim was sitting and said, "You may stand up and say it."

I looked around and saw Big Jim standing up straight and tall, and his jaw was set like he was thinking and he said in a polite but very firm voice, "May I have the note, Mr. Black? I'm the leader of the Sugar Creek Gang—and that's one of our rules—no note-writing or -passing in school.

If you don't mind, the Sugar Creek Gang will discipline William Collins.''

It surely sounded funny to hear Big Jim call me ''William,'' and you could have knocked me over with a feather, the way I felt . . . It certainly was a swell idea, if only it would work.

''I'm sorry,'' Mr. Black said, ''but I insist on having the note. You may be seated.''

Big Jim didn't be seated. He kept on standing. Then he spoke again and this is what he said very politely, ''In the United States, we respect the personal property of others. Isn't that note William Collins' personal property?''

Say, Mr. Black didn't seem to like that. He said to Big Jim, ''You sit down,'' and I saw Big Jim's face turn as white as a new snowdrift. He kept on standing, and Mr. *Black* kept on standing, and they were glaring at each other like two angry dogs do when they meet for the first time and each one of them is trying to let the other one of them know *which* one of them is going to be the boss—only I knew Big Jim didn't want to be *any*body's boss, but only wanted what he would call ''justice.''

Then Big Jim said, ''I *will* be seated, Mr. Black. You have a right to tell me that because you are the teacher, but I respectfully repeat, *I think that note is William Collins' personal property!*'' Big Jim sat down, doing it in a kinda dignified way, like he was a soldier obeying an

29

officer. He sat there with his pencil in his hand, making little fierce jabs on the Golden Rod writing tablet on his desk, and I know he was doing what people call "doodling." I always liked to see what Big Jim's doodling looked like, 'cause he made the most interesting "doodles" of anybody when he was writing and making marks and talking to other people at the same time. He actually drew interesting pictures and didn't know he was doing it.

Mr. Black held out one of his big, pudgy-looking hands toward me and said, "All right, William Collins, I'll take the note NOW!"

Well, what was I to do? Big Jim was the leader of the Sugar Creek *Gang* and I had always done what Big Jim told me to. Mr. Black was the teacher of the Sugar Creek *School* and all of us boys were supposed to obey the teacher. Also, I had my Pop's orders to behave myself; and not only that, my parents had taught me that the Bible itself teaches that a Christian ought to obey those who have the rule over him. But the whole question that was mixed up in my red head— which wasn't thinking very clearly that day anyway—was, Who *did* have the rule over me—Mr. Black, or Big Jim?

I had my hand in my pocket, gripping the note tight, and wishing I could tear it up with one hand, but knew I couldn't.

Without knowing I was going to, I turned

around quick to Big Jim and said, "What'll I do, Big Jim?"

I noticed his face was still white, and I knew that if he felt like I did, he was trembling inside and was in the right kind of mood for a good fight; and if it had been another gang instead of Mr. Black which was causing all the trouble, there would probably have been a real old fashioned rough and tumble fight before noon . . . While I was turned around, I could see all the rest of the boys and the girls in that one-room school were feeling just as funny on the inside as I was. Some of the girls were crying a little—all of them except maybe Circus's sister Lucille, who didn't cry easy. Poetry had his big fat hands doubled up on the desk in front of him; Dragonfly's very small face looked even smaller and his mussed-up hair looked like it was trying to stand on end. He had an indelible pencil in one of his hands and without knowing what he was doing, he had its purple point pressed against his two large front teeth. Little Jim sat there holding onto his long, new yellow pencil, just like he does when we're out in the woods and there is danger or something and he holds onto a stick which he nearly always carries when we go on hikes. Circus's monkey-like face didn't look mischievous, and I could see the muscles in his jaw moving like he was almost wishing he could get into some kind of a fight with somebody.

Then Big Jim spoke, and there was what my Pop would call a little sarcasm in his voice as he said, "Bill, I think you'd better let Mr. Black have your personal property."

Well, you know my right hand still held onto that note which Dragonfly had written. All of a sudden I realized that it was not only Bill Collins who was in trouble but it was Dragonfly himself, the grandest little guy in the gang, except maybe Little Jim, and he was too little and too spindle-legged to take a hard licking such as a man teacher might give him. While I was trying to make up my mind whether to do what Big Jim said, Mr. Black glared down at me with his jaw set and said very firmly, "It's the last time I'm asking you, William Collins! Give it to me NOW, or take the consequences!"

Well, I didn't know what the consequences might be, so I pulled my hand out of my pocket and tossed the folded-up note onto the teacher's desk.

Say, that really must have proved to him I *was* a rough-neck, for he turned as quick as a flash, and said, "Stand up, William Collins! And *get* the note, and *hand* it to me." Which, for some reason, I did almost right away.

He stood there, the folded note in his hand, behind his big desk, and looked out over the schoolroom through his thick-lensed glasses, and said, "Students of the Sugar Creek School, the leader of the Sugar Creek Gang is right. This note *was* the personal property of William Collins. However, since it was passed contrary to the rules of this school, it now belongs to me. Also since Roy Gilbert *wrote* the note, I'll ask *you* to stand up, Roy!'' He looked straight over to where Dragonfly was sitting. Say, I hadn't heard Dragonfly's real name for so long, I hardly knew who Mr. Black meant, until I saw Dragonfly jump like he was shot, shuffle to his feet, and stand looking down at his hands. He was actually shaking, 'cause he knew what I also knew, that the note was making fun of Mr. Black's bald head.

"You can come to the platform, Roy," Mr. Black said, and his face was very set.

"Ye-yes, sir," Dragonfly said, and started to shuffle down the aisle past the first grade girls near the front, and to the desk . . .

"You wrote this note, Roy?" Mr. Black asked.

Dragonfly's voice was trembling so bad it was pitiful. "Y-yes, s-sir!" he stuttered, and his voice certainly didn't sound like a rough-neck's voice, not nearly as much as Mr. Black's did, when he said, "*All right,* you may read it to the school!"

3

SAY, I tell you I felt sorry for little Dragonfly as he stood there beside Mr. Black's desk, while different girls in the room were half crying and while all of us were feeling like maybe we'd never felt before in all our lives. We'd never had much trouble in the Sugar Creek Gang school, on account of, as you know, our teachers had all been lady teachers and we had liked them.

All the time I was imagining what Dragonfly would see the very minute he unfolded that note, and it would be, "Some men have their hair parted on the left side, some have it parted on the right, some have it parted in the middle, and still others have it DE-parted in the middle . . ."

I happened to look at Shorty Long right that minute—and I had to look right across the top of Circus's ordinary-looking sister's head which had a pretty blue hair ribbon on it. And do you know what? Shorty Long's fat face had a funny look on it. He was looking straight at me and there was a half sneer on his face which seemed to say, "Smarty, you guys are going to catch it now. I

34

wish it was *you* up there, Bill Collins. You ought to have your ears boxed again . . .''

Maybe I just imagined that half sneer on his face was saying that, on account of my not liking him a lot. Then I looked at Dragonfly and he was getting ready to do what Mr. Black had told him to do, and that was to read the note out loud to the whole school!

Say, that little guy unfolded that note like it had a snake in it or maybe kinda like a girl would have opened it if she was afraid there might be a live mouse wrapped up in it.

Then, Dragonfly held the paper out toward the window like he couldn't see very well, and blinked his eyes, and started to move over toward the window.

At the window he strained his eyes again, and rubbed first one of them and then the other. Well, it would have been funny if it *had* been, but wasn't, although it was a little bit.

All of a sudden Dragonfly looked up and out the window, in fact all of us did, 'cause right that second we heard sleigh bells coming down the road. Say, if there's anything in all the world that sounds prettier than anything else it's the sound of sleigh bells across the snow! Even while we were having all that trouble, I felt sorry for the people down in Cuba where we'd all been just a week before on our Christmas vacation 'cause they never have any snow nor any sleigh bells.

Mr. Black's voice broke into my thoughts like a big finger being poked into a pretty soap bubble, when he said, "All right, Gilbert,"—meaning Dragonfly—"you may quit stalling! READ the NOTE!"

Dragonfly strained his eyes again, swallowed like a scrawny-necked chicken does when it is trying to swallow something too large for its thin neck. Then Dragonfly looked at me like a sick chicken, as much as to say, "Well, here goes . . . Sink or swim, live or die, survive or perish."

He also reminded me of a boy in swimming, getting ready to duck himself, and he takes hold of his nose with one hand, gets ready, shuts his eyes and plunks himself under.

All the time the sleigh bells were getting closer and closer, in fact they were coming very fast straight for the schoolhouse. In fact also, right that minute I looked past Dragonfly's head and saw two frisky, high-stepping horses hitched up to a big bob-sled come swinging through the open gate into the lane that runs along the edge of our schoolyard and turn again and come dashing, with bells ringing wildly, right straight toward our woodshed and the big maple tree . . .

Dragonfly swallowed again and strained his eyes at the note, just as a great big man's voice outside called to the horses and said, "Whoa!" which is what you say to horses you are driving when you want them to stop . . .

Well, we couldn't have heard Dragonfly anyway, and besides not a one of us wanted to. All of a sudden when I looked out of the window, I saw the horses pawing and prancing in a very proud way, and their bells were jingling and jangling and the man was calling, "Whoa, Blixen! Whoa there, Donder!" Blixen and Donder being the names of two of the reindeer in the poem called "The Night Before Christmas." I looked at Poetry, who always liked that poem so well and his lips were already moving and I knew that if we'd been somewhere else and he had had half a chance, he'd have been saying,

" 'Twas the night before Christmas when all through
   the house,
Not a creature was stirring, not even a mouse . . ."

Say, that's a great poem. I had even memorized it my lazy self. Anyway, those sleigh bells saved Dragonfly's life, or his skin maybe, 'cause, right that minute, Mr. Black said, "Quick, everybody in your seats. We're having company . . . Act natural. Start studying!"

Well, it was natural for some of us to start studying, and for some of us it would have been more natural for us to *stop* studying; but I was all thrilled inside, 'cause right that second I heard a musical woman's voice, and something inside me just started ringing like sleigh bells. It made me feel so good I could have shouted out-loud but I didn't dare. I knew though that if I'd been outside I would've, 'cause the musical lady's voice I'd heard was the pretty voice of our pretty other teacher who we'd all liked and who had gotten married while we were on our vacation in Cuba—and shouldn't have—anyway she shouldn't have without maybe asking the Sugar Creek Gang what we thought about it.

All of a sudden, Mr. Black cleared his throat, loud enough to be heard above the noise of the jingling sleigh bells and the other noise in the schoolroom, such as the shuffling of feet and the closing of books and the sniffling of Dragonfly who had a cold—Dragonfly nearly always having a cold in the winter, and hayfever in the summer, and nearly always having one of his Pop's big red bandanna handkerchiefs in—and also out of—his pocket . . . Just looking at Dragonfly's red bandanna handkerchief right that minute reminded me of what had happened down in Cuba, and for a half jiffy I could see Dragonfly down there, sneezing and sneezing and sneezing and I could see—and *smell*—the big brown billygoat down there and Old Man Paddler's lost twin brother.

But say, my thoughts came back in a flash to our one-room school where they also were anyway, and I heard out teacher say, "Attention, everybody"—meaning all of us please keep stiller than we were, as he might have something important to say. He said:

"Students of the Sugar Creek School, I want all of you to act as if nothing has happened . . . We've planned a little surprise for you all today—a bob-sled ride at the noon hour. ATTENTION!" He raised his big voice, and lowered his big bushy black eyebrows at the same time, and said, "Some of you boys don't deserve this surprise—," Then he stopped and looked straight toward my desk where I was sitting, and for some reason I was chewing gum—not even realizing I was doing it, although I knew it was maybe against the rule to chew gum in school . . . Anyway, I'd read a lot of advertisements in newspapers and magazines which said that chewing gum was very good for your nerves. And I really felt nervous that morning, what with getting my ears boxed and getting called down, and with all the excitement and everything else that was going on, and also all the trouble I'd had at home that morning, and with my Pop planning to give me a licking that night when I got home from school and everything . . . So without hardly knowing I was going to do it, I had taken some gum from Circus who had slipped it to me very quietly just a jiffy before and I had it in my mouth chewing it vigorously, not intending to chew it that way. Right that second Mr. Black, with his eyebrows down and his voice up, half thundered to me,

"William Collins! TAKE THAT GUM OUT OF YOUR MOUTH!"

Well, it wasn't funny, but almost half the school snickered, even some of the girls, only they didn't have time to laugh, on account of Mr. Black shushed them and said, "ORDER!"

Right away there was a little order.

Then he said, "Lay aside your work!" which most of us did, the rest of us having already laid it aside.

Then he said, "I want absolutely perfect behavior on this sleigh-ride. Understand?" He glared at us, and we understood.

Then he said, "Everybody wear your coats and caps, and don't act like a tribe of wild Indians . . ."

Boy oh boy, oh boy oh boy oh boy! It was going to be more fun than you could shake a stick at—our bob-sled ride with our pretty other teacher and also with her husband, who lived about a mile up the road from the schoolhouse and was a farmer, and who all of us boys knew and liked, most farmers being very fine people. The only thing was, we had all been kinda mad at him for marrying our teacher . . . Maybe he was going to try to make up for all the trouble he had caused us by taking us for a ride . . .

Anyway, boy oh boy oh boy! We were really going to have fun . . .

Well, I hadn't anymore than got my gum out

of my mouth, than I heard a sort of a hiss beside me and it was Circus's hand passing something to me—a folded piece of paper which looked like the one Dragonfly had had a jiffy before which was my personal property being given back to me. So just as quick as I could get the gum out of my mouth, I did, and wrapped it in that note, smashing it in good and hard, so as to make the gum stick to it, and also to make it hard for anybody to ever read what Dragonfly had written.

Then, school being dismissed, there was a sound like a barnyard full of chickens and hogs and cattle and barking dogs, as most of us made a dive for our wraps at the back of the schoolroom and for our coats and caps and boots and rubbers—the girls going almost as noisily as the boys—most girls acting like boys do anyway, my Pop says, until they are a dozen years old. Then some of them start acting like girls, which is just as bad.

Boy oh boy! *A bob-sled ride!* . . . With a whole gang of laughing, yelling, talking, screaming boys and girls!

4

HAVING a bob-sled ride with the Sugar Creek Gang and with all the rest of the Sugar Creek school, is almost the most fun a guy and his gang can have. In about seven minutes nearly all of us had finished eating our lunch, most of us still chewing the last three bites after we were all finished . . .

Say, I never saw a man teacher act so polite in my life as Mr. Black when we were having company. You would have thought all the school of us had been perfect all morning, the way he talked to Miss Brown whose name wasn't Miss Brown anymore but was Mrs. Jesperson, which is a Scandinavian name, and means she had married a Scandinavian, which *Mr*. Jesperson, her husband was, only we all knew him as Joe. He was a very polite person and when he talked, it sounded like he was singing a song which didn't have any tune, but only rhythm.

Anyway, pretty soon all of us had scrambled into that great big wagon box, and had settled ourselves down on the straw and blankets and were all yelling and talking and laughing and saying such things as "Ouch!"; "Hey, sit over!"; "Get off my foot!"; "That's *my* stomach you're walking on!" and things like that, when Mr. Black told us all to keep still a minute which we did for a *half* a minute, and he said to Mrs. Jesperson, our pretty lady other teacher, "I can understand, Miss Brown—I beg your pardon, Mrs. Jesperson—why you liked the pupils of the Number Nine school. They are a grand bunch and I'm sure we'll have a very happy half year together."

Well, it sounded very polite and for a minute I looked from where I was sitting beside and behind different members of the gang in the front of the wagon box to see if he really meant it. His voice was *very* polite as he finished.

But, for some reason, the words "half year" sounded like an awful long time to have to go to school yet before it would be out and the Sugar Creek Gang would be free to go galloping up and down Sugar Creek, along the paths, barefoot, and having fun again . . .

"I'm sure they *are* a grand bunch, as you say, Mr. Black," Miss Brown—I mean *Mrs. Jesperson*—said. She smiled, but before her smile had finished itself, her brown eyes were looking straight into her Swedish husband's greyish-blue ones and *he* was getting the tail end of her smile instead of Mr. Black.

"I'm sorry I won't be able to go along," Mr.

43

Black said. "I have some work to outline for the seventh grade. Be sure to have everybody back by one-thirty."

Poetry, beside me, said, "Hey! He's giving us an extra half hour!" which he was, and which was the first thing I'd noticed about our new teacher that made me think maybe I was going to like him a little bit, even if he *had* boxed my ears instead of Shorty Long's, and even if he wasn't a good enough citizen of the United States to respect the personal property of others.

Well, several times during that ride when I looked up from where I was sitting, to our pretty lady other teacher and her husband, I noticed they were looking at each other like they thought each other were the most important people in the world.

The Sugar Creek school had itself scattered all over the big wagonbox which was filled with oats straw, and blankets, and lap robes and car rugs.

Pretty soon we were off—with the horses prancing and with Mr. and Mrs. Jesperson sitting together at the front and the rest of us behind them and with *Mrs.* Jesperson helping to drive a little, and with the sleigh bells jingling and jangling and all of us yelling and hollering and calling to each other and laughing and having a great time . . .

It was while we were on that bob-sled ride that Shorty Long said something that made me not like him even worse than I did. There were all

kinds of interesting things to see along the roadside and on the different farms we passed, such
as horses and cattle and sheep and hogs and trees
which, with so much snow on them, looked like
great big white ghosts. Snowdrifts were piled
everywhere, looking like a lot of big rocks and
little hills with white blankets on them . . .

Poetry who is very good in arithmetic was
making up problems all along the way and count-
ing cows and sheep. When we passed Mr.
Jesperson's farm, there were a lot of cows standing in the barnyard so very close together, and so
many of them that it looked like there were maybe
a hundred altogether. Our horses were going so
fast and everybody was yelling and talking so
loud that I could hardly hear Poetry say, "Look,
there are seventy-nine cows!"

I looked and we were already passing the big
red barn, so I said, "You can't count that fast.
They're too close together to count 'em!"

"There were seventy-nine," Poetry said, and
he sounded so sure I almost believed it . . . Right
away we came to another farm, and there were
what looked like maybe a hundred hogs and sheep
and cattle all in the same big barnyard. Poetry
nudged me and looked out at the animals and
said, "See, Bill, I'm really *good* in arithmetic
. . . There are twenty-seven sheep, thirty-four
cows and fifty-three hogs."

"You *can't* count that fast," I said, and Little

Jim piped up and said the same thing, and so did Dragonfly, who was always very *poor* in arithmetic.

Well, we were coming to another farm where there were a lot of Holstein milk cows out in the barnyard, Holstein milk cows being black and white cows which give lots of milk but which doesn't have as much cream on it as the milk of Jersey or Guernsey cows does.

There looked like maybe thirty cows, but as fast and as carefully I counted, I couldn't possibly be sure how many there were . . .

But Poetry piped up and squawked in his duck-like voice and said, "There are thirty-three Holstein cows, and in the pen, beside the silo—" a silo being a tall round cylinder-shaped thing as high as a barn that you keep ensilage in to feed horses and cows and pigs with—"in the pen, beside the silo," Poetry finished, "are forty-one pigs."

"Keep still!" I said to Poetry. "Don't remind me of school. I want to forget it."

Circus looked at me, I being all slouched down on one elbow and said, "Hey, Long, sit up!"

And I yelled back at him, for he was sitting up pretty straight against the corner of the other end of the wagonbox, and I said, "I'll *sit* up if you'll *shut* up!" only I wouldn't, and I didn't, but I knew Circus was only kidding me.

In a few jiffies we would be coming to the

Collins' farm, and my Pop's cows and sheep and horses and hogs would be out there for Poetry to count. Boy 'oh boy, it always felt good to get near our house. The great big red barn, the old iron pump at the end of the walk not far from the kinda ordinary looking house, and the great big walnut tree close by, where in the summer-time the gang had a big high swing, the woodshed—just looking at the woodshed, though, gave me a homesick feeling, and almost right away I didn't feel very happy . . . Especially because right that minute, Shorty Long, who was sitting beside Dragonfly talking Openglopish with him, raised his voice and yelled to me, "Is that where you live, William?"

I didn't want to answer at all, and I didn't, but somebody else's voice did—some girl's voice, I think it was, but I couldn't tell whose it was, said, "Sure, that's where he lives."

Then Shorty Long yelled out loud enough for everybody to hear it and said, "In that funny looking little red house?" and he pointed toward our red-painted woodshed where my Pop was going to give me a licking that night when I got home from school.

I was boiling inside at him anyway for calling me William and for reminding me of Mr. Black and of my ears getting boxed, when he said, "Look, girls, there's where William Collins lives—in that little red house . . . Some boys'

47

fathers keep them in the woodshed so much they actually *live* there.''

I knew my face was as red as my hair, and it was just too bad the distance between me and Shorty Long was too long for one of my already-doubled-up fists to reach his fat jaw.

"Hey! Look!" Poetry said, gesturing toward our farm with one of his hands and saying with his duck-like voice, "There are three cows, twenty-four pigs, and thirty-eight sheep!"

Well, I happened to know that that was exactly right, 'cause I knew how many cows and pigs and sheep we had, but I also knew Poetry *didn't* know 'cause my Pop had just bought a lot of sheep. So I said to him, "For once you're right. But how can you tell?"

A half dozen others of us all of a sudden spoke up and said, "All right, smart guy, how can you count so fast?"

Then Poetry laughed and straightened up and said, "Fish—I knew you would bite on that nice fat worm. It's as easy as pie to tell how many farm animals there are in a field or pasture, or barnyard, if you know your arithmetic. You just count all the legs, and divide by four, and you have the answer."

* * * * *

Well, I have to admit, Poetry's joke made me feel like a fish, all right, and I also have to admit that it was funny.

"You didn't make that one up yourself," I said to him, and he said, "Nope, I just read it in a magazine!"

And Dragonfly who hadn't been getting any attention, but had spent most of his time on the ride talking to and listening to Shorty Long—both of them talking Openglopish—all of a sudden swished his Pop's great big red bandanna handkerchief out of his pocket and started in to sneezing—he actually sneezed six times in a row and said, "Thopis cropazopy opold opoats stropaw! OpI'm opallopergopic topo opit!" which in our language means, "This crazy old oats straw! I'm allergic to it." And it looked like he was.

Miss Brown—I mean, Mrs. Jesperson—wasn't helping drive right that minute. She was, in fact, looking at all of us like she thought we were the grandest gang of school kids she ever saw, which maybe we were, she not having taught school in any other school; then she said, "How did you like Cuba, Roy?"—meaning Dragonfly. "Were you allergic to anything down there?"

"He was allergic to *everything*," Little Jim piped up and said.

And Shorty Long, trying to say something bright, and not saying it, said, "He was so uppish, he turned up his nose at everything!" which maybe *was* a little funny, but not much.

In a few minutes the horses were started up

again and were going like a house afire down a nice pretty little hill. A jiffy later, we crossed a narrow iron bridge which spanned a small stream of water which was named "Wolf Creek." Then we went on up a hill on the other side, and all of a sudden we came to a pretty white church at the top of the hill on the left side, which was the church of all the Sugar Creek Gang and most of their parents went to every Sunday and also in the middle of the week on prayer meeting night. Right across the road from the church was a great big country schoolhouse which had two rooms in it and also had two teachers, and almost three times as many boys and girls went to it as went to our school.

Seeing a whole lot of boys and girls outside reminded us that it was still the noon hour. The boys and girls were playing in the church yard which was almost twice as large as the big school yard which we played in at our school. They had a great big circle out there and were playing what is called "Fox and Goose" in the snow, which is a game we all have a lot of fun playing at our school too. Seeing the church must have reminded our pretty lady other teacher of some of the short Christian choruses which we used to sing in our school, she being an honest-to-goodness Christian schoolteacher, and liking the gospel songs very much and also having a good singing voice. Real cheerfully she said, "Let's sing a chorus for the boys and girls out there," and right away she started to sing one which we all liked very much, and which our school used to sing for opening exercises.

As soon as she started it, I looked over at Shorty Long to see what he would think about it, not knowing whether he believed in songs like that and being almost sure he didn't, on account of him not acting like the kind of person who would like them. I studied his face a jiffy to see what he was thinking. Almost all of us were singing noisily, and also a bit bashfully, and also enjoying it, mostly on account of our liking our friendly other teacher so well. We liked the song even better 'cause we liked her. I also liked it better 'cause I thought Shorty Long didn't.

Well, he *really* didn't. He just sat there looking glum and bored and looking around at different ones of us to see if there was any of us who didn't like it either, and all of us did. He also looked like he felt more important than any of the rest of us, and it looked like he was looking at different ones of us to see if any of us felt as "uppish" as he did, and none of us did. So he was the only one who wasn't trying to sing except Dragonfly, who didn't have a good voice and who was what is called a "monotone," which means his tones were all on the same pitch and sounded like a small frog croaking along Sugar Creek in the summer-time.

Well, there was something awfully nice about a whole gang of boys and girls singing that chorus like we used to do when we had our other teacher, especially at the noon hour once in a while. One of the reasons why we all liked Miss Brown—Mrs. Jesperson, I mean—very much, was 'cause she not only claimed to be a Christian but she acted like one, kinda like one of the peach trees in my Pop's orchard, which was not only a peach tree, but actually had big, luscious peaches on it every year. She also understood us boys, not getting mad at us if at any time we made a mistake, and not always looking for somebody to blame something on. For a jiffy I stopped singing when I noticed Shorty Long looking disgusted and was grumbling to Dragonfly at the same time, and I got my ear close and heard him say, "It's sissified! It sounds like a lot of pigs squealing. Who wants to have a Sunday School all the time!"

Dragonfly got a funny look on his face which I'd never seen there before, and all of a sudden I had the queerest feeling around my chest. It was a kind of a scared feeling as if maybe Dragonfly was *believing* Shorty Long. I looked at Big Jim's fuzzy mustache, and at his face, to see what he thought, he being the leader of our gang; and right away I felt better, 'cause he was singing along with all the rest of us, only he was doing it more dignified, on account of being older. I noticed he was watching our minister's daughter, Sylvia, who was the oldest girl in the sled and also maybe the prettiest and she was singing too. I kinda felt that Big Jim liked the song better 'cause she liked it.

Poetry was squawking along beside me in his half-boy, half-man's voice. Circus's extra sweet voice sounded good. Little Jim's was like a little musical mouse's voice.

Well, Dragonfly still had that queer look on his face like he was ashamed of all of us, or something, or else he couldn't stand to be made fun of by Shorty Long. Right away I knew Shorty was what the Bible calls "tempting" Dragonfly to be ashamed of being a Christian and also right away I didn't like Shorty Long even worse.

I noticed something else too, and that was that Shorty Long was showing something to Dragonfly secretly, something printed on a piece of paper. He was holding it behind his coat and he and Dragonfly were looking at it.

Just then Dragonfly looked at me and he had the queerest look in his eyes . . . Then both of them started to talking Openglopish, which none of the rest of us knew well enough to understand. I could *talk* it pretty well, but couldn't *hear* it half as good, and they were talking it so fast . . .

I had a feeling that whatever they were talking about, it wasn't something I would like if I heard it—and then I saw it wasn't only something printed they were looking at, but there were some drawings which I got just a glimpse of before Shorty Long saw me looking and shoved them inside a brown envelope; also there was some printing at the bottom of the drawings which he was reading in Openglopish to Dragonfly, and Dragonfly still had that queer look on his face like he was doing something he oughtn't.

Well, there must have been some boys who attended that big two-room other school who felt as uppish as Shorty Long looked right that minute and who didn't appreciate good music, or else they were just like ordinary boys, who, the minute they saw anybody going past in the winter time, wanted to throw snowballs at them, 'cause right away some of those boys stopped playing and dashed out of their Fox-and-Goose ring toward the road and started scooping up great big handfuls of snow and making hard snowballs and throwing them toward us, which they shouldn't have on account of they might hit our horses. Right away I felt like I wanted to have a good old fashioned snowball fight, and right away I wished that the horses would stop and we could all jump out and have one.

It was easy not to get hit 'cause all we had to do was to duck down into the wagon box, and the snowballs would either fly over our heads or hit the side board or somewhere, anywhere except hit us. Before I could get down though, one hard snowball crashed against my shoulder and our teacher commanded, "Quick! DOWN—all of you, so you won't get hit!" And every one of us ducked, while a whole flock of snowballs went swishing over our heads, like a flock of white pigeons flying over our barn.

Then all of a sudden, I felt myself being jerked and jostled and all of us bumped into each other, and the sleigh bells on our horses started jingling and jangling and acting like they had gone wild and I heard Mr. Jesperson yell to the horses, "WHOA! . . . STEADY, BOYS!"

But his voice didn't do any good. Also I could see him pulling hard on the lines he was driving with.

Say, our team of horses must have been hit with a half-dozen hard snowballs by some of the boys who couldn't throw straight, or else the boys had thrown at the horses on purpose. I began to be excited, not even thinking of being scared at first when the team started running down the road as fast as they could, with Mr. Jesperson holding onto the lines as tight as he could and pulling and calling "WHOA!"

At the same time, our pretty lady other teacher was holding onto her husband, and the horses were acting like they were terribly scared. In fact, the sleigh bells were making enough noise to scare any horses into running away.

I had seen a runaway once, a team hitched up to a wagon, with nobody in it, running down the road as fast as they could go, looking like they were going maybe thirty or forty miles an hour, which is terribly fast for a team of horses and a wagon. Almost right away we came to a road that turns south and our team decided to turn down that road, which they did, and our big sled slid and skidded around the corner terribly fast. Before we even had time to get scared any worse, the back of our sled flew around with a grinding noise and swished into a deep ditch where there were a lot of snowdrifts.

It is a funny feeling, being scared, and not having time to think and not being sure whether you are in danger but knowing you are, and hoping you won't get hurt, and wondering if you will, and thinking about your Mom and Pop and your baby sister Charlotte Ann, and wondering if you'll get hurt bad enough so you'll be knocked unconscious and won't see anybody for awhile.

Most of the girls began to scream and scream and scream, like they were already terribly hurt, and the next thing we knew—that wagonbox skidded off its foundation into the deep ditch, and turned upside down with all of us in it, and also with some of us being dumped out of it at the same time.

The next thing I knew, I couldn't see anything on account of I was underneath the wagonbox which was upside down and I was under it, and it was dark. I could hear kids screaming all around me and I wondered if anybody was hurt, and hoped nobody was, not even me. And I knew it was an accident.

5

WELL, there we were, many of us under that upside down wagonbox—some of us under it, and some of us outside in the snowdrifts, and all of us making a lot of noise. I could hear kids screaming all around me, and because so many of us were almost scared half to death, I was a little bit scared myself.

I guess it was a good thing there were a half dozen great big fluffy snowdrifts there, 'cause it turned out that there wasn't a single one of us got hurt, except maybe just a few of us . . . Big Jim had a scratch on the back of his hand which wasn't bad, and which Sylvia's Mom dressed right away, our sled having been kind enough to turn upside down almost right in front of our minister's house; and Sylvia's Mom put a little antiseptic, called "merthyolate," on the hand and then tied it up with a bandage.

Sylvia's Pop came out to help turn the wagonbox right side up again. Almost in a few minutes there were a half dozen neighbor farmers around there, and most of the kids from the other school.

The men put the wagonbox on again, Joe Jesperson having stopped the horses almost right away after the accident, the horses not having run away like I was afraid they would.

Well, it was something to be thankful for. Sylvia's Pop, who is one of the best ministers we ever had, and who preaches all his sermons from the Bible, told us we ought to be thankful, which we ought. Also Sylvia's Pop was the kind of minister who was always looking for a chance to tell people things about the Saviour, so he asked everybody to be quiet a minute.

I was kinda glad he was there, 'cause I'll have to admit I was all trembling inside, and I knew I must have been more scared than I thought I was. He was not only a very human being who liked boys, and had laughed and laughed when he found out none of us were really hurt, but he said to all of us it would be a good time to stop and give thanks to the Lord Himself for having spared us all, and do you know what? Right out there along that roadside with all the farmers there and nearly all the kids from the other school and both their lady teachers there, every single one of us bowed our heads, and Sylvia's Pop said, "I don't believe it's too cold to ask the men if they will take off their hats while we pray."

I knew he was giving us boys a compliment when he didn't say "the men *and boys* take off their hats," but he called us all *men*. I took off my brown fur cap, Little Jim took off his small reddish cap, Big Jim took off his grey cap which had a long black bill that was broken, Circus swished off his very old blue cap which didn't have any ear-muffs on it but was large enough to be pulled down over his ears, Poetry took off his brown fur cap, Poetry and I liking each other a lot and whenever we could, buying hats and clothes alike. Dragonfly's cap was already off and he was knocking the snow out of it and off it, and Little Tom Till, who I hadn't paid much attention to, but who was also a member of the Sugar Creek Gang, had his cap already off and his red hair which was as red as mine, was all mussed up and powdered with snow.

Anyway, we all took off our hats, and caps, the farmer-men also, and there, while the sleigh bells were jingling a little every time the horses moved a little, Sylvia's Pop shut his eyes and lifted his kind face up toward the grey sky, and prayed.

Say, it was maybe the nicest prayer I think I ever heard. About all I can remember of it was, "Dear Heavenly Father, we thank Thee for the boys and the girls of America and of the whole world—boys and girls of every color and country; and right now especially, for the boys and girls of Sugar Creek. We thank Thee for having brought us all safely through this accident without anyone being seriously injured. We thank

Thee for having given the Lord Jesus Christ to die upon the cross of Calvary to be the Saviour of anybody and everybody who will believe in Him with all their hearts. We pray that if there are any among us here today who are not yet saved, very soon they will open their hearts to the Saviour and let Him come in . . . May any who may be blinded by unbelief, have their eyes opened . . .''

Hearing Sylvia's Pop say something about open eyes, made me want to open mine to see if Shorty Long had his eyes shut, like you are supposed to have them when you are praying, and so I opened mine quick, and looked quick over to Shorty Long, and would you believe it?—his eyes were wide open and he was just staring at the minister like he thought he was some queer animal or something.

We were all ready to go again, with all of us in the wagonbox, when all of a sudden Shorty Long said, "Hey, wait a minute! I've lost something!"

Before the horses could start, he climbed out over the side of the sled and was out in the snow, looking around to see if he could find something which he said he had lost.

Poetry who was standing beside me, nudged me in the ribs so hard it almost made me yell, and whispered to me, *"Sh! I've got it!"*

Well, you can believe me that I kept still— whatever it was that Poetry had. It made me feel good to know that he had something Shorty Long

61

was looking for. Shorty kept looking all around in the ditch, in the snow, and different ones of the gang, except Poetry and I, got out and tried to help him. All the time I was wondering what it was Shorty Long had lost and Poetry had found. Dragonfly, who who still had a funny look on his face, also was helping Shorty Long look for whatever it was.

"Did anybody find anything?" Shorty Long asked loud enough for us all to hear. "I lost—" and then he stopped whatever he was saying, and didn't finish his sentence.

A jiffy later when Shorty Long's back was turned to us, Poetry who had his back turned to Shorty Long and to the rest of everybody, half opened his coat and showed me the tip of a brown envelope in his pocket.

Boy, I had a funny feeling in my mind about that time, wishing I would get a chance to see what Shorty Long had been showing Dragonfly, and knowing that we couldn't keep it, 'cause it was Shorty's personal property. Pretty soon Poetry would have to tell Shorty Long he had it, and would give it to him.

All the way back to the Sugar Creek school, while we were all having not quite as much fun as we had had before the accident, I had what my Pop would have called a "premonition," which means that I had a feeling inside of me that the brown envelope which Poetry had in his pocket had a secret in it that was very important.

62

As I've already told you, every time a new boy moved into our neighborhood, we had to find out two things about him, and he had to find them out also. First, he had to find out right away whether he was going to run the gang or whether he was just going to *try* to; and the other thing that had to be decided was, could he *join* the gang— We had two or three good rules for anybody who could become a member of the gang, and one of them was that a boy couldn't be a liar, and another one was that he had to be respectful to his parents, and even if he wasn't a Christian he couldn't make fun of people who went to church. He was also supposed to go himself, even if his parents didn't go—which lots of parents don't, and should.

As you maybe know, if you've maybe read some of the other stories about the Sugar Creek Gang, about half of us were not Christians at first, Little Jim having nearly all the real religion there was in the whole gang, but most of us got to be saved. Dragonfly was the last one of us to be saved, except Little red-haired Tom Till, whose father was an infidel and whose mother had never had a chance in life to be happy, which is maybe one reason why Little Tom Till's big brother, Bob, had turned out to be such a bad boy, it not being easy for a boy to become a Christian unless his Pop is one too, on account of most boys do what their Pops do, and don't do what their Pops *don't*.

Well, as I said, I must have had a premonition, on account of I kept feeling all the time that there was something very important on the inside of the envelope. Pretty soon we got back to the school. Maybe I'd better tell you that while we were on the way, some of us talked to Mrs. Jesperson and said, "We don't like our new teacher. We'd rather have you again!"

Say, she just smiled at us, and called us all to attention, and while the horses were trotting along and the sleigh bells were jingling and jangling, she said to us, "Boys and girls of the Sugar Creek school":—

Everything was quiet for a minute except for the sound of the sled runners in the snow, and the bells ringing, and except also for Dragonfly's sneezing which he was doing again, on account of his still being allergic to the oats straw in the wagon. Most of the straw got dumped out in the accident, but enough of it was still on our blankets and rugs to make Dragonfly sneeze.

Then Mrs. Jesperson said, "Mr. Jesperson and I are going to be missionaries as some of you know. That's the real reason why I was led to resign from teaching. Also, some of you know that I have already finished my missionary training.

"You will be interested to know that our good friend, Mr. Seneth Paddler, whom you boys affectionately call 'Old Man Paddler,' has undertaken the support of both of us, while we are on the mission field.''

Mrs. Jesperson waited a minute while a lot of us asked questions, and then just as we were getting close to our school again, she said, ''Some of you have said you don't like Mr. Black. But I'm sure you *will* like him just as soon as you get better acquainted with him. Be sure to obey him in everything and be as kind and gentlemanly as possible. I am sure you will have a very happy year together. Remember that he does not know you as I have known you, and at first he may not understand you. Please be loyal to the principles of the Sugar Creek school which have been yours for years.

''I think it was very generous and thoughtful of Mr. Black to let us have this time together, also I think it was very courteous and thoughtful and unselfish of him to let me have you all to myself for this farewell visit together.''

Just about that time I began to feel a great big lump of something in my throat, being very sad that I was not going to get to see her again for a long time, not being sure I liked *Mr*. Jesperson very well, for marrying her and taking her away from us, and also I felt for a second or two that I might get to like Mr. *Black* a little bit, and I made up my mind that I was going to try to be even a better boy than I was.

Well, I won't take time to tell you right now

about how sad we all felt and that some of the girls cried and hugged Mrs. Jesperson. None of the Sugar Creek Gang were little enough not to feel bashful if we'd done it too, so we just shook hands with her instead.

All of us went back into the schoolhouse, and school started and lasted until recess, without anybody getting into any trouble, and Mr. Black behaved very well, for a new teacher.

At recess, which would last for fifteen minutes, we planned to have a gang meeting, which we did have in the woodshed, with Shorty Long not being allowed to come inside. In fact, Dragonfly wouldn't come in either, when he found out we wouldn't let Shorty Long in, and it looked like for the first time we were going to have trouble in our own gang.

I felt pretty terrible when the gang shut the door, and hooked it on the inside, and I knew that somewhere out in the schoolyard Shorty Long and our Dragonfly were talking Openglopish and maybe talking about us, and it looked like Shorty Long was going to break up our gang if we didn't do something about it. I couldn't help but feel that there was something in that brown envelope which would be very important. In fact, it might be so important that it would, whatever it was, cause us a lot of trouble.

6

IT WAS kinda dark in the woodshed with the door shut, on account of there not being any window. All the light there was came in through a crack up near the comb of the roof at the other end, just above the top of the big pile of wood which was piled high against the wall on that other end.

Big Jim sat down in front of us on a block of wood and the rest of us sat on a long bench which used to be a recitation bench in the schoolhouse itself. There were also two or three battered-up desks in the woodshed, some of them with initials carved on the tops by maybe some boy who should have known better. Right that minute I was looking at one of the desk tops and it had B.C. on it, which are my initials which stand for *Bill Collins*. I could hardly believe my eyes when I saw it, wondering who had done it, hardly remembering whether I had done it or not, and sort of remembering maybe I had, but that was a long time ago when I was little and didn't know much better.

Well, Big Jim called the meeting to order, and said, while all the rest of us kept kinda quiet, "All right, Poetry, let's have a look at Shorty Long's personal property."

Big Jim's saying that made me remember what had happened that morning in school, and my ears started to burn where they had been boxed.

Big Jim took the kinda smallish brown envelope which Poetry handed him, and sat very quiet for a jiffy, looking at the outside. Then with a dignified voice, like he was a judge in a courtroom or something, Big Jim said to Poetry, "You found this in a snowdrift, is that right?"

"Yes, sir," Poetry said.

"Has anybody seen this before?" was Big Jim's next question, and I said, "Yes, sir, I saw it."

"Where?"

"I saw Shorty Long showing it to Dragonfly while we were in the sled just before we had our wreck," I said.

"Have you seen the *inside* of it?" Big Jim asked.

"Not yet," I said, meaning I wanted to see what was in it right away.

Big Jim sat there with a puzzled face for a minute, while we waited for him to decide what he was going to do. At the same time he was doing like boys nearly always try to do when they are sitting on something that isn't very solid, or isn't fastened to the floor—he was sort of balancing himself on the standing-up block of wood, kinda like he was on a three-legged chair, one leg of the chair being the block of wood he was half sitting on, the other two legs being his own which were in front of him.

Big Jim held the envelope up, so the light from the crack in the woodshed behind him would shine on it, then he shook it, and I could hear it rattle and it sounded like a package of watermelon seeds in an envelope which my mom sometimes buys at a seed store in town in the spring.

Then Big Jim got a sober face, and said, using very dignified words like he was talking to dignified people, which he wasn't, "As much as I would like to open this and see what is in it, I cannot do so, because as was decided in school session this morning, Personal Property is personal property—"

Poetry snickered in a very undignified way, at that remark, but several of us shushed him and he kept still, and Big Jim went on . . .

"On the other hand," Big Jim said, still talking like we were dignified people, "if we did not know whose property this was, it would be lawful to open the envelope and examine its contents and—"

Well, for once I'm glad that even though Big Jim was talking in a very dignified voice, he wasn't sitting in a dignified way on that block of wood. He was, in fact, maybe without knowing he was going to do it, every now and then lifting both feet off the woodshed floor and trying to balance himself on the rather thin block of wood. Anyway, Poetry being very mischievous, and not being able to help it, all of a sudden let one of his big feet shoot out in front of him and give the block of wood a shove, and all of another sudden there was a scrambling shuffle which ended in Big Jim's being upset and tumbling over in several different directions at the same time and landing in a very undignified sprawl at our feet.

It was actually funny, and we started to laugh, until I saw what had happened. Say, he reached out with his hands in several different directions at the same time, to balance himself, and didn't, and the brown envelope got turned upside down in the shuffle; and, right in front of my eyes, I saw everything that was in it scattered over the woodshed floor . . .

Well, there was the personal property of Shorty Long right in front of the eyes of all of us, and it was a lot of pictures about the size of Kodak snapshots of a small size, and also what looked like a boy's drawing of several persons, which, now that we'd been in the dark awhile and could see better, I could see, and I saw my name at the bottom of one of the drawings, and it was spelled "*PILL* Collins."

Well, I remembered what Shorty Long had

called me that morning on the way to school, when he said, "From now on your name is just plain Pill Collins, *Pill,* as in caterpillar."

In about less than a jiffy, Big Jim had scrambled to his feet, and all those pictures were in one hand and the brown envelope was in the other—that is, all except that drawing with my name on it, which somehow I had picked up myself and was looking at, and I tell you that what I saw made me feel hot all over, it made me so mad at Shorty Long . . . I can't even tell you what the drawing looked like, except that it had a picture of somebody who looked very homely, and my name was under it and I was carrying a dinner pail which was colored with red crayon, and beside me was a very homely girl who was named Lucille Brown, Circus's sister. And right below my name were some words in quotation marks which meant I was supposed to be saying them, and they were terribly filthy words, even dirtier than the mud in our barnyard looks in the spring after a lot of hard rain.

Then, right beside my picture I saw one that was just as homely and it had Big Jim's name under it, and beside him was a girl . . .

I didn't get to see what the words were under Big Jim's name 'cause Big Jim took it and looked at it quick then shoved it and everything else back inside the envelope, like it was something especially dirty and he didn't want to even touch it.

Right that second I heard a snow ball go ker-wham against the woodshed door, and then another and another and another and before I could think what I was going to do I yelled, "Hey you, out there! *Stop* it!" I was out of my place in a fierce hurry. I leaped to the woodshed door, unhooked it, shoved it open and looked out to see who had dared to attack us.

The very second I opened the door, one of my eyes got pasted shut with a snow ball, which before it struck me I could see had been thrown by a great big fat lummox of a guy whose name was Shorty Long.

Well, I'd had one fight with him before Christmas, and he had licked me for awhile, and I had had another one that very morning, on the way to school, and had licked *him,* so I knew I could do it. And since I was already mad at him and since he had just pasted me ker-wham in the face with a snowball, I was still madder, especially on account of what was in the brown envelope, so I made a dive for the snow with both hands, made a hard snowball real quick, dodging several of his at the same time, and the fight was on. I threw my ball whizzety-sizzle toward Shorty Long, who ducked behind our snow fort which the gang had made beside the big maple tree that morning before school had started. My ball hit kerthud-wham against the front of the fort.

"COME ON, GANG!" I yelled to the guys

behind me, who were already tumbling out of the door at my heels. "Let's wash his face with snow. Let's beat up on him!"

Shorty Long was already interrupting what I was saying, so maybe the gang didn't hear me, and he was yelling, "William Collins lives in the woodshed! William Collins lives in the wood-shed!"

Right away all of us, and even Little Jim who liked to be kind to everybody even when he was angry at them, were on our way past the old iron pump not far from the narrow gate which opened into our school yard, right straight for Shorty Long's snow fort, which as I told you wasn't his fort anyway, but belonged to the gang, we having made it ourselves early that morning.

Before any of us got to the fort, all of us had thrown maybe a half dozen snowballs apiece, which we had made on the way, and also before we got there, Shorty Long had thrown several at us, one of which had hit me, kersmash-squish right in the face. Also Dragonfly was scooping up snowballs and throwing them at *us*. Imagine that! One of the members of the Sugar Creek Gang, playing traitor and throwing snowballs at the rest of the gang, and fighting against us! I could hardly believe my eyes—the one good eye that I had left!

Right that minute another snowball hit me kerthud-smash-squish right on the chin, and for a jiffy I couldn't see straight, so when I saw Shorty Long again he was holding both hands up to his face and over his ears and with the Sugar Creek Gang's snowballs pelting him all over, and he was running straight toward the steps and the door of the schoolhouse.

"He's going to tell the teacher on you," Dragonfly cried all of a sudden. His voice sounded like he wanted Shorty Long to do that and also wanted Mr. Black to take Shorty Long's part. Say, I grabbed up two or three hard snowballs from behind the fort which Shorty Long and Dragonfly had made them themselves, and had piled them up there while we were having our gang meeting in the woodshed. Boy, those balls were *hard*. I could tell that without thinking. I whirled and let them go with quick one-two-three, bang-sock-wham straight toward Shorty Long and the schoolhouse door toward which he was running, and—

Well, that's where even more trouble started. Right that minute, the only door the schoolhouse had burst open and one of my snowballs went whizzing in to smash ker-squash right in the center of Mr. Black's bald head, he having stooped at the very minute he opened the door to straighten the door mat.

Well, I felt a great big scare-stab of some kind in my heart. Imagine that crazy snowball missing Shorty Long and actually socking our bald-headed new teacher right in the center of his bald head!

I felt hot and cold and numb and everything. For half a jiffy I stood there, mixed up in my mind, then I turned and ran like a scared rabbit straight for the woodshed door and dived in, but before I could shut the door all the gang except Dragonfly was there scrambling in after me.

Panting and gasping for breath and sweating and scared, we slammed the door tight.

We stood there with our fists doubled up, trembling and waiting for *anything* to happen. It seemed dark inside again on account of our having been out in the bright light of the day for awhile.

"Sh! Listen!" Poetry said, which we were all doing anyway, but when he said that we listened harder, and sure enough we heard the schoolhouse door slam shut. Also we heard steps coming in our direction. I shoved Poetry aside and looked through a narrow crack in the door right next to the white knob, and sure enough it was Mr. Black. He had his big black fur cap on and his black overcoat which even while I looked at him, I thought would look pretty with about seven snowballs decorating it like a lot of white stars in the sky above Sugar Creek in the summer-time.

Maybe I thought that because I was seeing stars myself on account of Shorty Long's snowballs in my face.

Say, I never saw a man's face so set and so mad-looking in my life, I thought. I turned around quick, looked up toward the two-by-six cross beams which ran across the middle of the shed about three feet above our heads, and wondered if it would do any good to climb up there.

"Sh!" Big Jim said. "Everybody keep still!" which we did.

Closer and closer those steps came straight for the woodshed door, behind which we all, except Dragonfly, were.

"All right, Gang," Big Jim ordered us, "everybody against the door! Brace your feet!"

And we obeyed Big Jim.

7

It's a queer feeling, being scared and mad and wondering what is going to happen, and what if it does.

Crunch, crunch, crunch, faster and faster those big heavy steps of our bald-headed schoolteacher came straight for the woodshed door, and all of us were right behind Big Jim and Circus who were braced against the door so nobody could get it open.

"Stop grunting!" Big Jim ordered some of us who *were* grunting. We were pushing so hard against the door, without needing to yet, the door being the kind that opened inside.

"There he is—Sh!" Circus said, who had his eye on the crack in the door. "Keep still!"

We kept still and waited and listened. I could hear all of us breathing and could hear my heart pounding. Little Jim had his two small hands up against my brown sweater, with his feet braced behind him, looking kinda pale. I felt sorry for him, 'cause he never did like to have any trouble of any kind and was a grand little guy and never would fight unless he had to, and was the best Christian in the whole gang and maybe in the whole world, and wasn't a sissy either, but could knock home runs on our ball team. He actually shot a bear once which would have killed all of us maybe if he hadn't. And the way he had fought once when a tough town gang had tried to lick the Sugar Creek Gang was something grand. He had a temper that was better than mine 'cause he didn't let it explode and wasn't always saying things he was sorry for afterward like some of us were some of the time.

"Hey! What's that?" Little Tom Till hissed— "What's he trying to do?"

We were still listening, and sure enough, we heard it. Mr. Black was fumbling at the lock of the door and at the latch. I could hear it—and then a funny feeling grabbed me as I heard something go "clickety-click-snap!" It sounded like a— and then I knew what it was. Even before I could say it, Poetry said it for me in his squawky voice, and it was *"He's locked the door! We can't get out!"*

The very minute Poetry said that, everything was quiet outside, except for one thing, and that one thing was heavy crunching footsteps going *away* from the door, going past the woodshed, down past the Fox-and-Goose ring which we had made in the snow in the west end of our big school yard.

78

Big Jim unhooked the door, grabbed the white door knob, turned it, and tried to pull open the door, and couldn't.

"Let *me* try it," I said, and he did and I did, and the knob would turn, but that was all. We all knew what had happened. Mr. Black had brought the big new Yale lock which we always used at night to lock the door so thieves wouldn't steal the wood out of the woodshed, and had locked us in!

And that's a funnier feeling than being mad and scared and wondering if you're going to get a licking.

"He's locked us in!" we all said almost at the same time.

And he really had. The only way we could get out now would be to break out, 'cause there wasn't any window in the woodshed, and we didn't dare break out 'cause that would be damaging school property, and we could have trouble with the law if we did that. So there we were, and what would happen next I didn't know.

"Hey! Gang!" somebody hissed to all of us. I looked around, and there was Circus, up on the woodpile which was piled high against the other wall, and he was up there looking through a crack out in the direction toward which Mr. Black's crunching steps had gone.

Say, you should have seen us all scrambling up over those different kinds of short fireplace logs—oak and ironwood and elm and sycamore and ash and willow and maple and all kinds of wood from the different kinds of trees that grew along Sugar Creek.

Up where Circus was and where we all were in less than several jiffies, there was a larger crack in the woodshed wall, and right away we all were looking through it to see what Circus saw. I could hardly believe my half-swollen eyes, but it was happening just the same. Our new teacher was actually cutting switches from the drooping branches of the beech tree which grew in the very corner of the school yard. All of the Sugar Creek Gang and a lot of other people had carved their initials on the bark of that old beech tree—beech trees being the kind of trees on whose bark you can do that.

Well, in my mind's eye I could see myself getting a licking—and maybe right in this same woodshed, which was about the same size and kind that my Pop used at our house when he had to do that to me—when I was littler and didn't know much better than to do things that made Pop have to give me a licking. I didn't mind my Pop giving me a licking once in a while, but I certainly didn't want any new man teacher to try it. Besides, I thought, our nice other teacher shouldn't have gotten married like that, while we were all away on our Christmas vacation without even saying anything about it to any of us, or asking us if she could.

Well, in almost no time at all, Mr. Black had two long, wicked-looking switches cut and trimmed and was on his way back.

"Quick," Big Jim ordered. "Everybody down against the door. He'll have to break the door down to get in."

We were all braced against the door, none of us making much noise. Almost right away we heard heavy steps in the snow, and they stopped right outside our door.

My heart was beating faster than ever and I could almost feel my red hair trying to stand on end under my fur cap, which was beginning to feel too hot—only it wasn't on, but was probably out in the snow somewhere.

Then I heard the teacher's big gruff voice calling to somebody and saying, "Will you go and ring the bell, please? It's already past time for school to take up."

Right away, I heard somebody call from somewhere near the school and say, "All right," and it was Shorty Long's voice. Then I heard the bell ring in the belfry of the schoolhouse. Then in my mind's eye I could see Shorty Long wabbling to his seat near the fireplace and I could see a bunch of girls including Circus's ordinary sister and different ones, go swishing to the door, and making a lot of girlish noise getting to their seats.

Then I heard Mr. Black's voice talking and at the same time heard a key in the lock, "You may come out now, boys, and get in your seats quick. It's already ten minutes past time for recess to be over. You may all come out except William Collins.''

Big Jim let the door swing open letting in some blinding sunlight, but none of us moved. Big Jim just stood there, with his fists doubled up. Circus stood beside him with his battered old cap on one side of his head looking very fierce, red-haired Tom Till stood still right beside Circus, Little Jim was standing close to Big Jim, and Poetry was in front of me. I was behind all of us, but wasn't hiding but the whole gang was sort of making me stay back—

"Well?" It was Mr. Black's big gruff voice. His shaggy black eyebrows were almost as long as my Pop's reddish-black ones, I thought, and when his face was set like that it looked fierce. I had my eye on the two long angry-looking beech switches which he had in his hand.

Big Jim spoke up then, and I was certainly surprised at the politeness in his voice, as he said courteously, "Mr. Black, none of us feel that Bill has done anything seriously wrong."

"What?" I thought, so loud it seemed as if I had spoken the word.

And then the teacher's gruff voice came again, and it said firmly, "You may *all* pass into the schoolhouse, *except* William Collins. You may pass in *now!*"

My muscles were tense, and not a one of us moved, not even Little Jim.

Well, I don't know what I would have done if I had been a forty-year-old man teacher with a gang of boys like that defying me. But anyway, I saw the muscles of his square jaw tighten, and I saw his arms move so that one hand was against his hip and he glared at us all and especially at me, I thought. Then he said, "All right, then, it's a licking for every one of you!"

Say, I got the surprise of my life right that minute, 'cause right away somebody beside me moved and the next thing I knew, that same somebody was squeezing through all of us to the front, and it was Little Jim. Right away, he piped up and said to Mr. Black, "Maybe if you'll give *me* a licking instead of Bill, maybe you'll let all the rest of us go free!"

Before any of us could realize what he was doing, Little Jim was out the door and standing in front of Mr. Black, with an innocent look on his face like he often gets, which looked kinda like one of the lambs in a Bible story book which my parents bought for me, and where a little lamb is cuddled up in the arms of the Good Shepherd and looking very kind and innocent and not afraid.

Say, things were tense for a minute. I was waiting for Big Jim to do something, or say something, but he didn't. He just stood there, and we all just stood there, like a graveyard full of different-sized tomb stones, I even feeling like a cemetery myself.

8

SAY, THE expression on Little Jim's face, as he stood there, looking up at Mr. Black, both of his little hands at his side, and his pretty blue eyes which were even bluer than the sky was right that minute, looking so innocent-like, made me have the queerest feeling inside. As I told you before, Little Jim was probably the best Christian in all the Sugar Creek Gang, and he was always saying and thinking things that were printed in the Bible and was always trying to act like a gentleman. When I saw that lamb-like look on his face, all of a sudden I remembered the Bible story about Somebody Who had come into the world from Heaven, and Who had never done anything wrong in all His life, and Who was accused of having done a lot of wrong things, but hadn't, and had had to go on trial in the middle of the night, and then in the morning, had had to carry a great big cross out through the suburbs of the great big wicked city of Jerusalem, and all the time He didn't say anything or complain, and also all the time, He was as innocent as a lamb.

And also the Bible says, that "as a lamb before its shearers is dumb"—meaning "quiet, not even bleating"—"so He opened not His mouth," and didn't say anything, but let the people nail Him to a big cross and hang Him up between Heaven and earth, and the Bible says that He died there, and was the "Lamb of God that taketh away the sin of the world."

Sylvia's Pop, our new minister, says that when He died on the cross He died for everyone of us, so that everyone of us can go free, and not have to be punished for our sins.

Knowing Little Jim as well as I did, and knowing that his parents were Christians and studied the Bible a lot like parents should, and knowing that Little Jim himself understood how everybody could be saved from his sins just by believing that Jesus actually died in his place, and by trusting in Him, I knew that Little Jim was probably thinking that very same thing right that minute; and that while he was standing there, looking so lamb-like at Mr. Black, he was actually thinking about that Bible story.

For a half a jiffy I even thought that the Lord Jesus had given Himself to die on the cross for even Shorty Long, for the Bible actually says that He died for *sinners,* and Shorty Long was certainly a pretty bad one. In fact, Bill Collins himself was, also.

Anyway, it didn't take me more than a half a

jiffy—in fact, even less than a *half* of a half of a jiffy, to think that thought. It went through my mind like a little whirlwind goes swishing through our back yard and picks up all kinds of leaves and things and then drops them again as it goes on across the road and through the woods toward Sugar Creek. So I dropped all those thoughts almost right away.

I knew I wasn't going to let Little Jim take any licking for me or for any of us, but do you know what? Mr. Black stood there looking down at Little Jim, as if he couldn't even believe his eyes, and certainly not his ears. Then he looked at all of us and his greyish eyes looked like he wasn't seeing any of us, as if he was thinking of something else. First he looked back at Little Jim, then he looked at the long beech switches he had in his right hand, and the way he looked, he looked like he was thinking and trying to make up his mind to take Little Jim up on the proposition and lick him for all of us.

I don't know whether what Little Jim said made him remember the story in the Bible or not, but he got a half kind look in his eyes and on his face for a minute, like he couldn't do anything wrong if he was thinking about that story, which maybe nobody could.

All of a sudden he looked away toward the maple tree at something lying there in the snow. My eyes followed his to see what he was looking at, and before I could even realize what it was, he turned and walked over toward it, and stooped to pick up something, and I couldn't even believe my eyes. It was the brown envelope which Big Jim had had and which belonged to Shorty Long and which had in it those pictures of us and the filthy things about some of the girls in the Sugar Creek school, and also had in it some other pictures that only filthy-minded boys would like to see and talk about.

Well sir, the very minute Mr. Black stooped to pick up that brown envelope, I realized that we didn't want him to see it. What kind of boys would he think we were, if he saw what was on the inside of that envelope! And so without even thinking again, I yelled out, "HEY! THAT'S OUR PERSONAL PROPERTY! YOU CAN'T HAVE THAT!" I dashed out across the snow toward Mr. Black, and made a dive for the envelope.

Imagine me saying and doing a thing like that! But I really was doing nearly everything wrong all day, which is what might happen to any boy who gets his day started wrong at home before going to school, which is why parents ought always to try to help a boy start off to school cheerfully in the morning, if they can, which my parents sometimes can't on account of it being partly my fault.

Well, Mr. Black already had the envelope in

his hand, and just as I made a dive for it, he turned his body and I landed ker-wham against his big fat hip, and also landed a jiffy later ker-crumplety-fluff in a snowdrift right beside him and in front of all the Sugar Creek Gang.

Before I could roll over and sit up and start to stand up again, I heard a lot of swishing footsteps and I saw something that looked like a flying boy, only it didn't have wings. It also looked like a boy on a football field, making what is called "a flying tackle."

Sure enough, that's what it was, only it wasn't any football game, for the next thing I knew there were seven of us all piled in that same big snowdrift, on top of and underneath each other, just like we were in a football game. It was Circus who had made the flying leap at Mr. Black's ankles, and bowled him over, and in a jiffy there were fourteen legs and fourteen arms and all of us all mixed up in a cold snowdrift, probably the biggest snowdrift in the whole schoolyard.

All of us were tangled up and were also trying to untangle ourselves at the same time, and I tell you it was a very cold and also a very hot time we were having. There was the sound of grunting and groaning and Mr. Black was half yelling, "Let me up, you little whippersnappers! Get off my chest! Let go of my leg! OH—Let me loose. O-O-O-OH!"

There was more grunting and groaning and grunting and groaning from all of us, the grunting coming from the Sugar Creek Gang and both grunting and groaning coming from Mr. Black. I had hold of one of his arms, the one that had the brown envelope in its hand. Poetry was lying across Mr. Black's chest in the white snowdrift, and only one of us wasn't in on the wrestling match, and that was Dragonfly who in a flash of a jiffy I saw standing there looking on with a very puzzled expression on his face.

Well, I don't think boys in a school ought ever to do anything like we were doing. There wasn't a one of us that had planned on doing it, and there wasn't a one of us that would have done it if we had thought first. There wasn't a one of us that would have been so disrespectful even to a teacher we didn't like. But it was already too late, and already being done, and there we were, holding him down and afraid to let him go, and we didn't know what to do. We'd probably all get a licking, although the way I felt right that minute, I wasn't going to let anybody give me a licking if I could help it.

I don't know what would have happened if something else hadn't happened but it did. I heard the sound of an automobile horn. As quick as I could, I looked to see who it was, and it was my Pop's long green automobile out in front of the front gate in the road.

Then I heard my Pop's great big voice calling out across the snowy schoolyard, "HELLO, EVERYBODY!"

Right away "everybody," which is us,—and especially me, Bill Collins—wondered what was going to happen next, and what if it did?

There we were, with all of us in a fierce wrestling match with a big schoolteacher in a big cold white snowdrift, with our reputation at stake, meaning, what if Mr. Black got that envelope of filthy pictures and words in it and thought it was *really* ours, and thought we were that kind of tough boys, which we weren't! We just didn't *dare* to let him have it. We had to get it away from him, which, all of a sudden, we did.

Almost before my Pop's big voice had finished yelling, "Hello, everybody!" Poetry hissed to me, "Hey, Bill, let him go! I've got the envelope!"

I looked as quick as I could and saw Poetry shoving something inside his coat pocket, and right away the fight or whatever it was we were having was over.

In a few jiffies we were all untangled from each other and Mr. Black was shaking out his fur cap which had come off in the scuffle, and was brushing off his coat and saying in a very pleasant voice to my Pop, "Mr. Collins! You caught us right in the midst of an old fashioned snow-fight."

My Pop was looking at different ones of us and especially at me, and probably at my one not-so-good eye, and listening to all of us panting.

"I suppose you've come to visit school, Mr. Collins?" Mr. Black said. "That's fine. Just come right on in—it's a bit past time for recess to be over, and some of the pupils are already in their seats."

"No, I can't stop now, Mr. Black," Pop said. "Mrs. Collins and I will both come and visit one of these days, though . . . I just stopped to remind Bill to hurry home right after school."

Pop turned to me then to finish what he wanted to say, and it was, "I'm taking your mother to Brown City. Your cousin, Wally, has a new baby sister, so Mother's going to help look after the house . . ."

"Will she take Charlotte Ann with her?" I asked, thinking of my pink-cheeked baby sister, Charlotte Ann, the grandest baby sister I'd or anybody'd ever had, thinking also of my red-haired cousin, Wally, and wondering if his new baby sister would have red hair, which mine didn't.

"Sure, she'll take Charlotte Ann," Pop said. "What'd two men do trying to take care of a baby girl?"

Before my Pop had finished what he was saying, he was striding on his way back to the car, half talking over his shoulder as he said one more sentence. "No loitering on the way, now, Bill," which was the same as saying that I sometimes did.

Then Mr. Black said, "I can release him right now, Mr. Collins, if you need him," which for some reason sounded to me like he would be glad to get rid of me, as I was probably causing too much trouble, which was probably the truth. In fact, it looked like I was the cause of nearly all the trouble our gang had had all day and it was all on account of Shorty Long.

I looked at Big Jim's fuzzy-mustached face to see what he thought, and also at Little Jim's lamb-like face, and neither one of them was telling me not to go with my Pop. I really wanted to go, 'cause I wanted to see Mom and Charlotte Ann before Pop drove them to the city. Besides I felt sure if I stayed, I'd get a licking from Mr. Black. The very minute Pop would be gone, Mr. Black would probably get over being polite, and trouble would start all over again. So if I left, most of the trouble would be gone. Besides I certainly didn't want any licking all by myself in that woodshed—

Thinking that reminded me that there was also a woodshed at home. If I decided to stay at school, when I did get home later, Pop would be gone and would probably not get back till away after dark, and by that time it'd be too

93

late to go out to a woodshed for a licking, maybe.

Well, I knew Poetry had the brown envelope safe in his pocket. Also, right that minute, Poetry called to Pop and asked, "Can Bill come over to stay at my house tonight?"

Pop stopped stock still, turned around and said, "That depends—I'll see what your mother says," he finished, talking to me.

Mr. Black took out his watch and looked at it, and said, "You might just as well ride along with your father, William. In fact, I think we'll dismiss early today, this being the first day after vacation and hard to get back into the swing of school anyway."

"All right then, Bill," Pop called, "get your lunch pail and come on! Your mother's waiting!"

I leaped into life and made a dive for the schoolhouse door to get my dinner pail which was on the long shelf that runs along the back wall of the schoolroom.

Well, the minute I stepped into that schoolhouse, I could hardly believe my eyes at what I saw. I looked right down the row of seats past the Poetry-shaped stove, and to the left, right where my desk was, and would you believe it? Most of the books were out of my desk and were piled on the top of it. In fact somebody was pulling books out of my desk, right that very minute, and it was Shorty Long himself, pulling the books out one at a time and looking inside of each one.

9

WELL, I don't suppose I was ever so tangled up in my mind in my whole life as I was right that minute, what with everything that had happened and was still happening and which was yet to happen before that day would be finished. I could hardly blame myself for what I did right then. I yelled to Shorty Long, in Openglopish and said, "Shoportopy Lopong! Gopet opout opof mopy dopesk!" which means in English, "Shorty Long! Get out of my desk!"

Say he jumped like he had been shot somewhere with a boy's sling; and without maybe intending to, he brushed against the stack of my books on my desk and they all went ker-whamety-flop-bang on the floor, getting there almost a half jiffy before Shorty Long did, who stumbled over them trying to get away from my desk, on account of I made a quick dive for my desk myself.

Also Shorty Long got to the floor just before I did, and for some reason both of us were into a rough and tumble scramble. I really didn't intend to have another fight with Shorty Long, 'cause

I'd had all the fights that day I wanted, but of course it looked like one. Right that minute I heard a saucy girl's voice from across the schoolroom somewhere, saying, "Bill Collins! Can't you live even one *minute* without getting into a fight!" And I knew it was the voice of Circus's ordinary-looking sister, and for some reason I began to feel even worse than I had already felt for some time anyway.

"I'm not fighting!" I barked at her. And it didn't seem like I was. I was just sort of wrestling with Shorty Long.

All of a sudden we let loose of each other and shuffled to our feet and stood panting and looking at each other, like two roosters do, when they've fought awhile and are resting and looking at each other and are getting ready to dive into each other again just as soon as one or the other starts the fight again.

"What'd you take my books out of my desk for?" I said to Shorty Long, and he said, " 'Snone of your business. I was looking for something important."

Then Dragonfly piped up from somewhere in the room and said, "He was looking for something he lost on the sleigh ride."

So that was it! Well, for some reason, I began to lose some of my temper. I said to him, "Oh well, that's different! Go ahead and look! Only I'd appreciate it if you'd put all my books back in

97

very carefully. Of course, I couldn't ask you to *think* of asking *permission* to get into my desk. I couldn't ask you to *think* at all, 'cause you can't! A guy has to have brains to do that!'' And with that remark, which I shouldn't have made, I whirled around, stooped, picked up my books myself and shoved them back into my desk, being only a little less careful than I always was when I put them in.

Right that second, I heard my Pop's voice calling from outside saying, "Hurry up, Bill!" which I did. There wouldn't have been any fun staying and finishing the fight even if it had been one, with nobody in that schoolroom boosting for me, or caring whether I got licked or not, so I shoved the last book into its place, dodged around the end of the row of seats and grabbed my dinner pail off the long shelf by the door, opened the door and yelled out to my Pop, "Coming!" and was quick on my way out to our long green car, leaving my troubles behind me.

The only thing was, though, I seemed to have a whole heartful of trouble inside me, too, 'cause I was very sad all the way home.

"Don't you feel happy, Bill?" Pop said to me as we were swishing along down the lane past one of our neighbor's houses—the only neighbor we had who didn't have any children.

All of a sudden when Pop asked me that, I felt a great big lump come into my throat. I blinked my eyes and looked away out through the frosted window. Not being able to see through it very well, on account of the frost, I rolled it down and looked out at the clean snow, with the pretty drifts, and at some of the big white blotches of snow which were like big clean packs of cotton on the fir trees, and for some reason I felt like I wasn't nearly as clean as the trees. In fact I wished whatever was hurting on the inside of me would quit so I could talk, but I didn't dare answer Pop on account of there were tears in my voice which I didn't want him to hear. Also, right that minute I saw our house and the red woodshed and right away I rolled the frosted window up again, just as Pop swung into our gate which he had left open . . . Our car made a wide circle around the drive, swished past the big plum tree and stopped right close to the water tank where we watered our horses. A whitish looking smoke was coming out of the little stove pipe of the oil-burning stove which was down in the bottom of the tank, keeping the water from freezing so our horses and cattle could have drinking water without our having to chop holes in the ice—in fact, sometimes in the winter it got so cold around Sugar Creek that our big water tank would freeze all the way to the bottom.

Right away Mom opened our kitchen door, and looked out and said, "Hello, Billy Boy," which I didn't like very well, on account of it sounded like I was littler than I was. In fact I didn't want to be called *Billy* anymore at all, but only *Bill* like other men are called whose names are "William."

I was already out of the car, so I kinda grunted back to Mom, "Hullo," and she said, "Why, what's the matter? Aren't you glad your cousin Wally has a new baby sister?"

I wasn't. In fact I don't know of a thing in the world that could have made me glad right that minute.

"Let's get going on the chores right away," Pop ordered me, and I started toward the house where I nearly always went first when I came home, to get a sandwich which Mom sometimes let me have, on account of I was always as hungry as the wolf that ate up Little Red Riding Hood's grandmother, right after school.

"Wait a minute, Bill. The BARN! We do the chores in the *barn*—not the house!" Pop said.

And because as I have already told you, I was feeling pretty sad, all of a sudden I wanted to scream, what with everything I had done or started to do all day had either been wrong or else someone had thought it was. I not only wanted to scream, but for some reason all of a sudden, I did. I screamed and screamed and screamed.

And Mom said, "What on *earth!*"

And Pop said, "That's a fine way to act when you can't get your own way. Any time we let you go again away down to Cuba by airplane, and have a good time. Young man, I'm afraid you're getting to be too independent. You're—"

Mom's voice cut in like she thought maybe we ought to change the subject, and so she asked pleasantly, "How did you like your new teacher today, Bill?"

"I *didn't!*" I said savagely, and shouldn't have.

"WELL!" Mom said, "You don't need to take my *head* off!"

It was only after I'd said it that way that I knew I'd said it savagely and right away I was sorry 'cause I had the best Mom in the world, and also the best Pop and I didn't believe in talking back to them or being sassy to them, so also right away I felt even worse.

"They were having a scuffle in the snow, when I drove up," Pop said to Mom, "and Mr. Black was so jolly."

I wanted to speak up and say, "We were having a *fight*," but I realized that that would be contradicting my Pop, which for some reason I didn't want to do.

But I was feeling worse every minute.

"What'll I do, first—" I said to Pop, "—throw down hay for the horses?"

"Nope, gather the eggs first before it gets dark. In fact, you'll have to have the flashlight even now. You can go in the house for that, if you want to," which meant I could probably get a sandwich while I was there, if Mom had one ready. For a minute though, I forgot that I'd come home early, and since Mom nearly always gathered the eggs herself in the wintertime before I came home from school, I said to Pop, "Aren't the eggs gathered *yet?* I thought *Mom* always gathered them!" and for some reason on account of my not feeling very good, my voice sounded cranky again and sounded like I was disgusted 'cause the eggs weren't already gathered and also disgusted because I had to gather them myself.

Anyway I made a real quick dash past our woodshed door, and was in such a hurry to get in the house and get the flashlight that I only gave my feet a couple of swipes on the doormat, but I hadn't any more than shoved the door open than Mom who had come outside, yelled to me and said, "Bill, wipe your feet carefully! I've just mopped the kitchen floor!"

I gave my feet maybe seven swipes apiece, and then swished into the house, shutting the door decently, and went around in different directions looking for Pop's big flashlight.

I finally found it in Mom's bedroom on the dresser, and while I was in there I saw my baby sister Charlotte Ann, sitting up in her baby bed which had a Scotch Terrier design on it, just like her bassinet had had when she was a little baby. She had her pretty blackish-reddish curls all brushed into a sort of a curl on the top of her head, and I could see that her face had maybe just been washed on account of it looked like it had had soap on it. Right beside her on a tall table was a bar of soap in a soap dish. Charlotte Ann had on what Mom called a "combed wool shirt" and different kinds of other clothes. Say, seeing me must have made her all of a sudden want to stand up, and so she scrambled and grunted her way to her feet, holding onto the bars of her tiny bed and standing right up on both her pink bare feet. Also right that minute, she decided she wanted to get *out* of her bed—and I at the same time decided that she ought not to. So I tried to make her sit down again. Also, right beside the soap dish on the table, was a bowl filled with steaming water which meant that Mom had been giving Charlotte Ann a bath, getting her ready to go along on the trip to Brown City to see Cousin Wally's new baby sister.

Well, that bowl of water shouldn't have been there right that minute. Anyway Mom probably shouldn't have waxed the hardwood floor of that bedroom, and there shouldn't have been a rug on it right where I was standing . . . Before I could even know what was going to happen, it had happened . . . Charlotte Ann caught hold of my flashlight which she had decided she wanted, and which was probably the reason why she had stood up in the first place, and I was trying to make her let go and to make her sit down at the same time . . .

"Hey, you!" I said. "I've had enough for one day. Do as I tell you, will you! Let *go!* You've got to learn to take orders if you want to get anywhere in this life! LET GO!"

I couldn't just *jerk* the flashlight away from her, on account of it would be rude, and also on account of it would make her cry. I'd tried that once before when I was taking something away from her and she had set up a howl worse than any two of Circus's Pop's big hound dogs make when they have treed a coon. So I just sort of tried to twist the flashlight out of her hand without hurting her, and I didn't know there was wax on the floor under the rug.

But there was, and ker-slipetty-swish-swoosh-BUMP, my feet went in one direction and I in the other. The table being tall and not very wide, my up-in-the-air feet got tangled up with it and almost before I hit the floor good and hard, the little table did the same thing; also the soap dish and the bowl of sudsy water did the same thing, just as Charlotte Ann screamed and just as Mom came hurrying in to find out what all the noise was about, and to say "BILL COLLINS! WHAT ON *EARTH*—?" which is what Mom sometimes says when such unearthly things happen.

Well, I can't even take time to tell you now, what else happened. I knew my Pop had already planned for me to spend some time in the wood-shed, and I hoped Mom would understand. I don't know what I would have done if I had been my Mom and had worked hard to wax the bedroom floor and then have an awkward boy upset a bowl of sudsy water on it and have the water go swishing in every direction there was; also if at the same time the very pretty bowl went kercrash against the floor and broke into maybe a thousand pieces, which it did. I certainly expected my Mom to make a lot of noise with her voice like she sometimes did, but instead I saw her face turn white like she was terribly afraid, or something, and she sort of lifted her hand to her forehead and swayed like she was dizzy. Then she reached out toward the ledge of the window that looks out on the road and the woods, and caught herself from falling, then she staggered over to the edge of the bed and sat down on the very pretty green and white chenille spread. She held her hand to her heart, which was probably beating very fast, and said, with a very kind voice that had a faraway sound in it, like she was talking to Somebody else and not to me, "That's another one of the 'All things,' I suppose."

"What?" I said, looking up at her from the floor where I was sitting.

My Mom still had a sort of faraway look in her eyes as she answered me and said, "I promised Him I'd trust Him."

"Promised who *what?*" I asked, glad if she

wanted to talk about anything else, and feeling absolutely terrible inside—*terrible*.

"I'll tell you later," Mom said . . . "You just run along and gather the eggs. I'll have this cleaned up in a little while."

Say, when I looked at my Mom's face, it had the kindest look I had ever seen on it except maybe that time when I had walked into that same bedroom the day after Charlotte Ann was born and saw Mom lying there with the new baby beside her, and her face had looked maybe like an angel's face looks, it was so kind.

I scrambled to my feet, feeling very queer inside, and liking my Mom a lot. I hurried out through the living room and also through the kitchen, not intending to stop to make myself a sandwich, but seeing one lying there on the work table beside the big water pail which always stands in the corner near the kitchen door, I knew Mom had made it for me, and I liked her even better.

Mom was right behind me getting the mop out of the broom closet and I heard her humming a song we used to sing in church. It made me feel queer inside, and also a little bit sadder, on account of I was sorry I had made such a mess for her to clean up, and also when I went out the door with the egg basket on my arm and Pop's flashlight in one hand, and was on the way past the woodshed, I remembered the words of the song which Mom was singing and they were:

106

"What a Friend we have in Jesus,
All our sins and griefs to bear;
What a privilege to carry
Everything to God in prayer."

Well, for some reason I began to get a warm feeling inside of me. I was real glad I had that kind of a mother, and I sort of knew that while she would be cleaning up the mess I had accidentally made, she would be humming that song all the way through, and also she probably would be thinking of the words; and Mom, being an actual, honest-to-goodness Christian, would probably be doing what the song said, that is, she would be praying.

I don't know why I hadn't thought of it before, but for some reason while I was up in our dark haymow, flashing the light into the dark corners where several of our old hens always laid their eggs, it seemed like Mom's idea was a very good one. I thought that even a boy ought to get down on his knees somewhere all by himself when he is having different kinds of trouble and actually pray about them. Once I'd heard our minister say that "Any old coward can mumble along on the Lord's prayer in church when everybody else is praying too, but it takes a real man to get down all by himself and pray to God all alone."

Anyway, all of a sudden, with everything in the world having gone wrong all day, and with my having lost my temper so many times and having also said a lot of things I shouldn't have, and with my Pop not understanding me very well, and going to give me a licking in the woodshed maybe in just a little while, and with my Mom being so kind to me and maybe right that minute was in the downstairs bedroom on her knees cleaning up my mess, it seemed like I ought to be brave enough to pray right that minute.

Besides, that hen's nest was right under the big cross-beam that had the crack in it where a long time ago I used to put my New Testament while I was waiting for Circus's Pop to be saved. Anyway, without hardly knowing I was going to do it, I had my hat off like our minister had had us all do along the roadside that day, and I was down on both of my knees in the sweet-smelling alfalfa hay right beside the hen's nest.

It only took me a jiffy to say a few words, but all of a sudden I began to feel very quiet inside of me and to love my Mom and even my Pop a lot. I also loved the One I was talking to and for some reason I thought maybe it wouldn't be so bad to have a licking even if I hadn't done anything wrong on purpose.

While I was on my knees, I heard a noise outside our barn up near the house. I looked out through a crack but didn't see anything, so I just sort of looked at the pretty snowdrifts that were piled around and along the old rail fence across the road from our house, and at the pretty woods with all the trees without any leaves on them, and my thoughts went racing down the old footpath which we boys always raced on in the summer and which led straight for Sugar Creek, and the spring, and along the shore to the old swimming hole where we all had so much fun swimming and diving in the summer-time. On especially hot days when we were dusty and sweaty, it felt good to get nice and cool and clean again; and without knowing I was doing it until I *heard* myself doing it, I was singing another hymn which my Mom liked so well, and it was:

"Whiter than snow, yes whiter than snow,
Now wash me and I shall be whiter than snow."

I was just starting to reach down and pick up two snow-white eggs out of the nest when I heard somebody behind me clearing his throat. I jumped like I was shot, and looked quick, and it was my Pop, who had climbed up the haymow ladder and was looking right straight toward me.

I wondered if he had seen me, or maybe heard me, and I wished he hadn't even though I knew my Pop prayed himself sometimes right up in that same haymow, but for some reason I wished he hadn't seen me if he had.

"Hi, Pop," I said cheerfully, but with my

heart pounding fast. I picked up the two eggs with one hand and put them in the basket.

"Hi, Bill," Pop said back to me. "Want to throw down the hay for the horses—a little of each—clover and alfalfa?"

"Sure," I said. "There were two eggs in this nest today! Do you suppose maybe old Bent-comb laid two in one day?"—Bent-comb being the name of our old white leghorn hen which laid her eggs up there, her long red comb being very long and was all bent over and hung down so low on the left side that it half hid one of her eyes.

"Nope," Pop said, "one of those eggs is a glass egg which I put there this morning, just to sort of remind Lady Bent-comb when she comes up that it's a nice nest in which to lay her egg. Then she won't go off and start a new nest somewhere where we'll have to hunt for it."

I put the glass egg back into the nest, set the basket down in a safe place, and reached for the pitchfork to throw down the hay, when Pop said, "I'll take the eggs to the house, Bill. You feed the horses, and then come on up to the house as soon as you can. We want to get that woodshed business over as soon as possible."

Pop took the basket and climbed backwards down the ladder, whistling a tune of some kind, and it sounded like the one I'd just been whistling myself.

10

"Woodshed business," was a funny way to say it, I thought. I knew my Pop was right and that we had better get it over with as soon as possible. But even though I felt a lot better on the *inside* of me, I knew that pretty soon I wouldn't feel very good on the *outside;* it didn't feel good either to know that my Pop didn't like me any too well and that he thought I needed a licking, which maybe I *didn't*. I couldn't tell for sure, 'cause Pop nearly always decided that himself. In fact I hardly ever felt like I needed one, even after it was over with.

It only took me a very few jiffies to get the hay thrown down for the horses, and to put it in their mangers for them to eat, and then to get started on the way up the snowpath to the house. In fact, even as slow as I tried to walk, it seemed like I was getting there too quick.

I sort of circled around the woodshed a little, having to wipe extra snow off my boots before I could get into our kitchen door, which also took a little more time but not much.

It was while I was sweeping that snow off with a broom which Mom always kept at our back door in the winter-time, that an idea came to me which I'd read somewhere in a story, and that was that it wouldn't hurt so much to get licked if I had more *clothes* on. I knew that I had a heavy pair of corduroy trousers upstairs in my room, which I could go up and put on if I had time enough—slipping them on under the trousers I already had on, and then the licking I'd get pretty soon wouldn't be such a noisy one. Pop never liked to have me make much noise while I was getting a licking.

As quietly as I could, I slipped into our kitchen door, realizing right away that Mom and Pop were in the other room somewhere with Charlotte Ann, and maybe Pop was looking at what had happened to the waxed bedroom floor and maybe he and Mom were talking about *me* and what I had done, and a lot of other things I had been doing all day and why. Anyway, right away I was creeping stealthily up our carpeted stairway. Pretty soon I was around the corner of the bannister and in my own room where I took down a wire clothes hanger, on which I had actually remembered to hang my corduroy trousers the last time I had taken them off.

I had to be very quiet 'cause there was an open register in the floor of our other upstairs room which was used to let in warm air in the wintertime from the warm living room downstairs. My trousers weren't only about half on, when I thought I heard something that sounded funny, in fact I heard my name and without realizing I was doing what is called "eavesdropping" and that maybe I shouldn't have done it, I sneaked very quietly into that other room and leaned over and listened. In fact, I was leaning over at just about the *same* angle I *would* be leaning again in the woodshed in maybe a few more jiffies, I thought.

Say, strange things were going on down in that room. There were my Mom and Pop standing together with my Mom's pretty grayish brown hair leaning up against Pop's right shoulder, and he was leaning down to her with his face kinda buried against the top of her head, and I could hear my Mom crying a little. I could also hear her saying in a half-muffled voice to my Pop, "Of *course*, I care that it happened. That was such a lovely bowl—the only heirloom from my grandmother I really ever liked, and of *course* I care that my nice waxed floor is all spoiled, but—" then Mom stopped talking and my Pop leaned down and kissed her pretty grayish-brown hair and sort of whispered something I couldn't hear and wasn't supposed to anyway, and then Mom went on in a tearful voice that also sounded kinda happy and this is what she said, saying the same thing she had said to me before, and it was, "But I promised Him I'd trust Him, and I suppose this is one of the 'all things.' "

"I guess it is, Mother," I heard Pop say, and then I knew they liked each other a lot, but I couldn't help wondering what they meant by "all things." Maybe they meant that everything I ever did was wrong or ever would do was *going* to be wrong. Right away I heard Pop say, "But we have to be sure we love him," and Mom said, "I know it. Sometimes I don't think I do—not nearly enough."

"I'm afraid I don't either," Pop said, and it certainly didn't make me feel very good to hear that. Didn't my parents love me very much? Well, I could hardly blame them, I thought, and then I heard my Pop say something else that made me feel even stranger inside, and that was, "I'd rather take a licking myself than do what I have to do right now."

"What's that?" Mom asked, and Pop said, "I have to give our boy a licking out in the woodshed. I promised him one this morning, and—."

"Can't we forgive him this time?" Mom interrupted him and said, "I don't like to have it happen just before I go away, for a week. I'd feel terrible."

"So would I," I thought, but somehow for some reason it seemed like maybe I ought not to put on my corduroy trousers under my others, which I didn't. Instead I hung them back on the

114

hanger and started to whistle a little,—and it was the same tune my Pop had been whistling when he'd started to the house a little while before.

Right away I heard a voice call from down in that other room and it was Pop saying, "That you up there, Bill?"

"Yep!" I called back down cheerfully.

"Come on down here a minute." His voice didn't sound very cheerful.

In a minute I was down in the living room where Mom and Pop were, and they both turned and looked at me, with strange expressions in their eyes, which seemed to say, "Well,—"

"Let's get it over with," I said to Pop, and he and I went out of that room into the kitchen and through it to the back door, and across the back porch, down the back steps, past the broom I'd use to sweep off the snow from my boots; then we passed the water tank where the white smoke was coming out of the stove pipe. In a very short jiffy we came to the woodshed, I following along not very far behind Pop. Say, that old door's hinges squeaked worse than I'd ever heard them squeak before.

We were inside right away. It was a whole lot nicer woodshed to get a licking in than the one we had at school. It wasn't very dark inside, even with the door shut, on account of we had a glass window on the west side, which was the direction toward which there was going to be a very pretty sunset after a while and which I always liked to watch. In fact Pop and Mom and I used to like to watch the sunset together lots of times when we all liked each other a lot and when none of us had done anything to make trouble.

But when I saw my Pop reach up to the top of a tool cabinet which he had on the wall and take down a couple of old beech switches, which he had used on me all the other times he'd had to give me a licking, I knew we wouldn't get to enjoy any sunset together that evening. I felt like Mom had said she'd feel—I hated to have such a thing happen just when she was going away, on account of I wanted Mom to remember me as being a good boy, and with all of us liking each other a lot like we nearly always do most of the time at our house.

I could see Pop's face with its big shaggy eyebrows which hung over his eyes like a grassy ledge along Sugar Creek. I looked especially to see if his teeth were shining under his reddish mustache and they weren't, so I knew he wasn't smiling.

Then Pop said to me, "Are you ready?"

I turned sidewise toward him and stammered, "Y-yes, s-s-sir!"

"You know you've done a lot of wrong things today?" I didn't know my grammar well enough to tell whether it was a question or a statement. I

116

remembered what Mom had said, and remembering all the things I'd done all day that had gotten me into trouble, I said, "Yes, sir." Some of them hadn't seemed wrong, but I *had* talked back to my parents, and that is wrong whether you do it on purpose or not. Also, somehow I seemed to remember Little Jim who had walked out of our woodshed toward Mr. Black today and he had looked as innocent as a lamb, and had seemed like he *wanted* to take a licking and let the rest of us go free. So, I just stood there, waiting, making up my mind there wouldn't be any noise.

Pop's voice sounded very kind as he said to me, "Have you anything to say in self-defense— whether you're guilty or not guilty?"

And I said to Pop, "I don't think I did anything wrong on purpose." When I said that, I really couldn't remember anything I had done wrong on purpose, and as I looked up at my Pop, it didn't seem right that I was going to get a licking.

Pop who had one of the switches ready, stopped and looked at it and then at me, and said to me, "Bill Collins, I've never yet caught you telling a lie. I don't believe you ever told me one in your life."

I remembered the story of George Washington who had cut down a cherry tree once, and had told the truth about it, and so what Pop said made me feel better.

"You really feel deep down in your heart that you haven't done or said anything wrong?" Pop said, and I said, "Not on purpose, but I know I've *said* things I shouldn't have."

Say, my great big Pop just stood there and looked down at me, and I could see his face and the muscles of his jaw working like he was thinking hard. Then I saw him swallow like there was something stuck in his throat, and he was having a hard time to get it down.

We just stood there, neither one of us saying anything. Then Pop all of a sudden turned and walked over to the tool cabinet and took out a hatchet which looked a little bit like the one I'd seen in that picture of George Washington and the Cherry Tree, and very carefully, without saying anything, Pop laid those two switches down on a block of wood, and right there in front of my eyes he took first one quick sharp stroke with the hatchet, and another and another and another and then another, cutting those switches into maybe a dozen pieces.

I don't think I ever felt so queer in my life, 'cause Pop had used those switches on me a good many times in my life, and to see him cutting them into little short lengths, meant they couldn't ever be used on me again. If he ever gave me a licking he would have to have something new to do it with.

Then Pop stooped, gathered up the pieces, and

tossed them into a little wooden box with handles on it which we used to put kindling wood in sometimes.

Without knowing I was going to say anything, I said to Pop, "Aren't you going to—to give me a licking?"

Pop straightened up and looked down at me, with his eyes almost looking straight through me, yet they had a faraway expression in them like he wasn't seeing me at all. I looked right straight into his steelish-grayish-blue eyes and kept on looking into them. Then he spoke with his jaw set tight, and the words sort of came out from between his teeth without his lips hardly moving at all, and this is what he said, "Bill Collins, right or wrong, I am going to believe you. Furthermore, as far as I am concerned, this is our last trip to this woodshed. Sooner than your mother and I think, you will be a young man . . . The days of whipping ought to be over with. I know it has sometimes been necessary in the past, but let's count the past forever past, Bill. Let's burn the switches tonight—and let's never again do anything that will make us have to cut another—shall we?"

I swallowed something that got into my throat, and felt like my Pop was the finest, most wonderful Pop in the world, and I made up my mind that he'd never have to cut another switch.

But I couldn't say a word. All of a sudden

Pop's big hand reached out toward me, and without stopping to think, I swished my hand out toward his and grabbed it, and the next thing we knew we were holding onto each other's hands real tight, like Poetry and I do sometimes when we make a convenant of some kind.

I tell you it was the grandest feeling in the world. I had the swellest Pop in the world, and right away me and Pop stepped out of the door into the weather, and the sun was getting almost low enough to set.

Pop said, "You can put those sticks in the kitchen stove, if you want to."

But I didn't want to. I stopped stock still, and looked down at my boots, and kicked a little snow off the walk, and Pop said, "No, I think I'd better do it."

With that, Pop turned and went back into the woodshed and shut the door after him, leaving me there all by myself. Right away I saw our snow-shovel leaning against the side of the wood-shed. Also I noticed, without anybody telling me, that there wasn't any path scooped from the side door to the other path I'd made that morning which led out to the front gate and to our mail-box, on which was Pop's name, "Theodore Collins."

I walked around under our grape arbor, and to the other side of the woodshed to where the snow-shovel was where Pop had left it when he had finished scooping a path out to our chicken house, and was about to take it when I heard my Pop's voice inside, and it sounded very queer, like he was almost crying, and before I could get the shovel and go away, I'd heard him say, "And please, God, help me to be a better father to my fine son. Give me the grace to forgive him as Thou didst forgive me for Jesus' sake . . . Make us comrades, make us pals, and yet help me to be a faithful father, firm when I have to be, and willing to forgive whenever grace is needed . . ."

For a minute as I hurried as fast as I could toward where the snow needed to be shovelled, I couldn't see very well, and I actually stumbled over the board walk that leads from the back door to the iron pitcher-pump near the water tank.

It was getting pretty close to supper time, I thought, already hungry—or rather, still hungry, in spite of the sandwich I'd had.

I felt good to think I'd thought of shovelling that walk myself, without being told to, and I hurried fast to get started with the job so Mom wouldn't think of it and tell me to do it first.

First I grabbed the broom from our back steps and went around to the side porch and started in like a house afire, sweeping off the steps. Then I worked my way out to the other path which I'd shovelled that morning to the mailbox. During the day quite a little other snow had sifted into that other path, so I swept it clean all the way out to the gate and around to the box.

All the time I was feeling fine, to know that everything was all right between me and Pop, but I was still a little bothered about Mom, and I couldn't forget that both of them had said they didn't love me as much as they ought, and I made up my mind that I would make them like me if I could.

I kept thinking about what Mom had said too about what I'd done being one of the "All things," and I decided that whatever she meant, this was *one* thing I could do that was *right,* and not wrong. Pretty soon it would be time to eat supper. In fact I decided to hurry and get the snow shovelled first and then hurry to the house and without being told to, wash my hands with soap and start right in setting the table. Also I'd ask if there was anything else I could do.

I was almost done, when I heard our woodshed door open, and I knew Pop had finished whatever he had been doing inside. Then he called to me and said, "I'll get the milking done, Bill, and we'll have supper right away. You can help your mother as soon as you've finished out there," —telling me to do something I had already thought of. Pop and Mom were always doing that, not knowing that sometimes I thought of doing things myself, but I didn't even get mad at Pop. I yelled back to him, "Oke-doke!" and

122

swished my broom around the gate a little, deciding that Pop had meant for me to stop doing what I was doing, that it wasn't very important and to go help Mom.

I wanted to help Mom, but I was still bothered about what I had done, and I hated to go into the house.

I swept off my boots good, went in, hurried into our bathroom and washed my hands even better than I sometimes do, and started in to setting the table. I noticed that Mom was very quiet, and that her eyes were red around the lids like she had been crying about something. But she was sort of humming a little tune. I also noticed that our box of kindling wood was already beside the stove, and that the little pieces of the beech switches were there on top.

When I got a chance I went into the other room where Charlotte Ann was on the floor with a stack of square alphabet blocks, piling them up and knocking them down.

Then I sort of eased into the bedroom where there had been the big accident and the floor was already as clean as it could be. I got a surprise when I looked on the wall just above Mom and Pop's bed and there was a brand new, very pretty wall motto which I'd never seen there before, and it had a Bible verse on it.

I just stared at it, remembering something, and wondering at the same time, and thinking and feeling better inside of me, when all of a sudden Mom came in and stood beside me and didn't say anything.

Neither of us said anything for a minute, then Mom said pleasantly, "Mr. Paddler stopped in today, and gave me that. Do you like it?"

"It's pretty," I said, which it was, all in some kind of fancy raised lettering on a beautiful bluish-gray background.

Then Mom said something I will maybe never forget, and it made me like her a lot, even better than I ever did, and this is what she said, "I've decided to make that my life motto. I know it'll help me to keep from worrying about things— such things as happened this afternoon." With that Mom turned and swished out into the other room, and through it to the kitchen, just as I heard the back door open and Pop come in, and shut the door after him. Right away I heard a cat mewing and I knew our old black and white cat had followed him inside, and was asking as politely as she could, for somebody to please hurry up with her supper.

I stood there looking at the pretty wall motto, which had shining letters on it and liked it a lot. I didn't understand it though until later on at the table, when we were having the blessing just before we ate, like we always do.

Say, all of a sudden I looked away from the wall motto, toward somebody that was coming up through the woods from Sugar Creek. It looked like a man in old working clothes. He kinda slipped along from one tree to another and from one bush to another, like he didn't want anybody to see him.

Then he stopped right behind the big cedar tree right on the other side of the rail fence just across the yard. My heart began to beat very fast and excitedly, and I felt inside of me that something was going to happen, just what I didn't know.

I stood there glued to my place, while Charlotte Ann started in fussing in the other room. Then the man in the old clothes slipped through the rail fence and glided along the side ditch right straight toward our front gate. I wondered if I ought to say, "Hey, Pop! Come here!" but I didn't. Instead I waited and I saw that man make a bee-line straight for our mailbox, open it and then close it again real quick like he'd put something inside, which he probably had.

The man sort of reminded me of Shorty Long, the way he walked, but he was somebody I had never seen before, only I guess I couldn't see him very well, on account of it was darker there by the woods than it was most any place else right that minute.

I had a feeling that there was something very important that somebody had put into our mailbox, and I started to trembling inside, 'cause right that minute whoever it was, turned and started like a flash and ran like one of the Circus's Pop's hounds runs after a rabbit which jumps up before him when he's nosing around a brushpile or somewhere along Sugar Creek.

In a jiffy I would have opened our front door and gone swishing barehanded out to the mailbox, but right that second Mom called from the kitchen where we were going to have our supper and said, "All right, Bill, bring Charlotte Ann and come on. Put her in her chair."

I don't know why I decided to keep still and not tell my parents what I'd seen, but I got to wondering if maybe there was something in our mailbox that was for me personally and that my parents ought not to see it till after I'd seen it myself.

So I decided to wait till after supper, then I'd go dashing out quick . . . It was a hard supper to live through, on account of my curiosity. I felt fine though the very minute I had Charlotte Ann in my arms and was starting with her to the kitchen for I heard the stove lid of our range being put back on like somebody had taken it off and put it on again; and when I stepped into the kitchen, I looked into the woodbox and the pieces of the beech switches were gone. I didn't even look at my Pop to see what had happened to them. I just felt like a million dollars about everything. Both my parents liked me again and also I had a mystery out in our mailbox waiting for me to solve the very minute I had a chance.

126

Just before we ate, we all sat very quiet a minute, Mom having a hard time to get Charlotte Ann to keep still long enough for any of us to pray; and also folding her hands for her like we were teaching her to do, it being good for all children to learn to be respectful to God, even before they know they are doing it, my Pop says.

Well, as I said, it was while we were having the blessing that I found out what my parents meant about ''All things'' and also what they had meant when they talked about not loving somebody as much as they knew they ought.

At our house we nearly always took turns praying at the table. Sometimes Pop prayed, sometimes Mom did, and sometimes I did, although I couldn't pray very well, on account of I had always said a little poem prayer since I was little and had just got started to adding words of my own. Anyway it was Mom's turn. We all bowed our heads, and this is what Mom said, ''Dear Heavenly Father, we do thank Thee for Thy wonderful love for us all, in giving Thy Son to die upon the cross for our sins. We do thank Thee that no matter what happens in life to those of us who love Thee, that 'All things work together for good to them that love God, to them that are the called according to his purpose . . !' ''

My thoughts kinda left Mom's prayer for a minute, and swished into the bedroom to where I had spilled all the water and had broken the pretty bowl and had spoiled the rug and the waxed floor, and in my imagination I was reading the pretty new wall motto which Old Man Paddler had given Mom that day and which had on it the same thing Mom had just said in her prayer, and I thought I knew why Mom hadn't worried too much about what I'd done . . . Then when my thoughts came back again to what Mom was praying, she was saying, ". . . And help us to love Thee more and more . . . We know we do not love Thee enough— none of us, but we *do* love Thee . . . Bless us all. Bless our son, Bill, and our blessed baby, Charlotte Ann, whom Thou hast given us to take care of, and bless all the boys of the Sugar Creek Gang . . . Be with Wally, too, and the new baby, and also bless this food for which we thank Thee . . . In Jesus' name, Amen.''

It was a grand prayer, and I knew that everybody in our family liked everybody else. It had certainly been a stormy day at our house and at school, maybe the stormiest day we'd ever had, with me being the center of most of it, but it was all over at last—that is, all over except my trip to the mailbox which I'd take in a jiffy.

''May I be excused?'' I said to Mom and Pop, as soon as I'd eaten a lot of supper, and Pop said, ''What for?'' and I said, ''Oh, I just want to go out doors for awhile . . . I'll be right back.''

"Certainly," Mom said, "but come right back, 'cause . . ."

Then Mom stopped, and I finished the sentence for her, " 'cause we want to get the dishes done before you go? Oke-doke," I said and felt just fine inside.

Out of doors, I made a bee-line for that mail-box which had the name "Theodore Collins" on it, every drop of blood in me tingling with excitement, and sure enough, right inside that box, was an envelope without any stamp on it, and it was addressed to "Mr. William Collins, Sr."

I'd never seen the handwriting before and I wondered who had written to me and why. Also I wondered what on earth the "Sr." was doing on the end of my name. Anyway, just like people do when they get letters, I decided to open it right away, which I did. Talk about a crazy letter. It had all kinds of misspelled words and absolutely didn't make sense in some of the things it said.

I started to the house, reading the letter on the way, when my Pop called to me from the porch, "Why don't you walk in the path, Bill?"

I stopped, surprised. I was clear out in the middle of our yard, walking in snow which was deeper than my ankles, and getting my trouser cuffs all wet and filled with snow.

"I've got a letter!" I yelled to him—"a crazy letter, from some crazy person."

By the time I had got back into the path again

129

and had walked in it to our back porch, this is
what I had read in some man's crazy handwriting, which was almost as crazy as Dragonfly's
had been that morning when he had written that
note about our new teacher's bald head. And this
was what I had read:

> "Dear William Collins:
>   Your son better treat my boy decent or I'll
> shake the living daylights out of him. It's a pity a
> family cant move into a naborhood without a
> gang of ruffnecks beating up on his boy . . . I
> don't know if you are the ones who took my wife
> to church last night or not, but somebody did
> while I was away from home and you can't
> believe a thing she says about me. You mind
> your own business and I'll mind mine. My wife
> has enuff high and mity ideas without going to
> some fancy church to get more. If she would
> obey her husband like the Bible says, it would do
> her some good to read the Bible, but she don't
> . . . Your boy is the worst ruffneck in the whole
> Sugar Creek Gang of ruffnecks, so beware . . ."

The letter wasn't signed and it didn't make
sense, 'cause I wasn't married and didn't have a
"ruffneck" son. I seemed to know it was written
by Shorty Long's Dad, but why should he write
it to me—but even before I got to the end of the
letter and to the water tank at the same time
where Pop was waiting for me, I guessed the

man had intended to write it to my Pop, thinking I was William, *Jr.*, and my Pop was William, *Sr.*, which is the way some boys and their Pops are named.

Just that minute, Mom opened the door and called, "Telephone, Bill. It's one of the Gang. Hurry up. He says it's something very important!"

On the way into our house with the letter in my hand, I kept wondering if it was Poetry and what if it was and what if he wanted to tell me something about Shorty Long and the very bad things he had said about us on the pictures he had drawn. Also I was wondering if Poetry wanted me to stay at his house that night, and if my parents would let me.

Also, I was just itching to tell him about the letter, and also I knew I could hardly wait to show it to Pop, thinking it was probably intended for him anyway.

Anyway, if the letter I had was from Shorty Long's Pop, which I knew it must be, then it explained a little bit why Shorty Long himself was such a terrible boy, most boys being bad 'cause their Pops didn't train them up in the way they ought to go.

But say, before I tell you about what Poetry wanted to talk to me about, I'd better get this story done in a hurry, on account of it is already long enough. As I said, it was the end of a very stormy day, the stormiest one I'd probably ever had . . . I won't even have time to tell you any more about Mr. Black, and about the fire in the schoolhouse, which I had planned to, on account of this story being long enough, but say, the way that fire got started was the queerest way you ever saw—what with Mr. Black inside with the windows shut and with some of us boys on the roof of the schoolhouse and with the ladder which we'd put up, fallen down, and I couldn't get off the roof without falling or jumping and maybe getting hurt.

But just as soon as I have a chance I'll get going on that next story and tell you all about it, and also about a lot of other important things that happened to the Sugar Creek Gang that winter.

The Chicago Adventure

Sugar Creek Gang

THE CHICAGO ADVENTURE

Original title:

Sugar Creek Gang in Chicago

by

Paul Hutchens

MOODY PRESS

CHICAGO

1

ROARING ALONG through the sky five thousand feet high—which is almost a mile—and at four hundred miles an hour, was the most thrilling experience of my life up to that time. Well, come to think of it, I guess riding on the waves of a mad lake with nothing to hold me up except a life-preserver vest, was the *most* thrilling, as well as the craziest. As I told you in my last story about the Sugar Creek Gang, being tossed around by those great big angry waves was like being scared half to death riding on a tiltawhirl at a county fair.

I had thought maybe an airplane ride would be even worse—or maybe better. It wasn't at all, but boy, oh boy! Was it different!

Of course none of us thought that Dragonfly, who is the balloon-eyed member of our gang, would get a bad case of vertigo and scare us all half to death and have to have the airplane's stewardess give him first aid to bring him back to normal again. In fact, the pilot actually had to come down from being almost two miles high

to a lower altitude before Dragonfly was all right.

That's getting too far ahead of the story though, and I'll have to wait a chapter or two before I explain what vertigo means. I'm going to be a doctor when I grow up, you know, and that's why I'm learning the names of all the medical terms I can while I'm little, which I'm not actually anymore. I'm already ten and three-fourths years old and have red hair and— But it wouldn't be fair to tell you about myself first before introducing you to the rest of the gang.

The Sugar Creek Gang is really the most important gang in the whole country, maybe. Anyway we have more twisted-up adventures than most anybody else in the whole world, and so far they have all come out all right.

Maybe I'd better take several jiffies right now to introduce you to the gang—or maybe I should say "introduce the members of the gang to you," and to explain why we were going to take an airplane ride and where to. You remember that Circus who is our acrobat and who also has an acrobatic voice that can climb the musical scale even better than he can climb a tree, had been invited to go to Chicago to sing over the radio in a great big church on Thanksgiving Day. Well, the date had been changed and he was going to go to sing at what is called a Youth Rally on Labor Day weekend instead, and all the gang was

6

going with him. Little Jim, who is the littlest and the grandest guy in the gang, and maybe in the whole world, *had* to go with him to accompany him on the piano anyway, he being an expert pianist. So, of course, we all wanted to go along, and our parents had finally said we could—that is, they had *finally* said we could. It took my brownish-gray-haired mom quite a while to make up her mind to let me go, and I had to wipe dishes every noon for all the rest of the summer just to show my appreciation. I even had to wipe them as if I liked to and didn't, although I was beginning to have sense enough not to say so.

The day Mom finally made up her mind was one of the hottest days we'd had that year. I actually never had felt such tired weather in all my life. You could lie right down after eating a dinner of fried chicken, noodles, buttered mashed potatoes and raspberry shortcake, and go to sleep in less than a minute, and stay asleep all the way through dishwashing time—that is, if Mom didn't get tired waiting for you to come and help, and call you. You could even sleep better if you knew that pretty soon, after the dishes were done, there were potatoes to be hoed and beans to pick. But if you happened to be going swimming, or there was going to be a gang meeting, you weren't even sleepy.

Well, that afternoon there were beans to be picked, so right away as soon as I had finished

7

my shortcake, I asked to be excused, and Dad said, "Yes," and let me get up and go into our living room which was the coolest room in our house and lie down on the floor until Mom had the dishes ready.

Mom's floor was always clean, but even at that she always made me lay a paper down on it before I could put a pillow down to sleep on. I hadn't any more than lain down, it seemed, when Mom's voice came sizzling in from the kitchen and woke me up. Say, I didn't any more like to wake up than I do any other time. I was dreaming the craziest dream I'd dreamed in my whole life. Anyway it seemed crazy at the time, and anybody would have laughed at it. I never realized while I was dreaming it, that it was going to happen almost like that in real life after we got to Chicago.

Anyway I dreamed that I was an actual doctor already, and that I was in a hospital with a lot of nurses in white all around, and also, all around and overhead airplane motors were droning. One of the members of the Sugar Creek Gang had eaten too much raspberry shortcake and had the stomachache, and the only thing that would help him was for me, the doctor, to give him what is called a blood transfusion, which I did without knowing how. In my dream I was pouring black raspberry juice into one of the veins of his arm through a little tin funnel, and he was crying and

saying, "I don't like to wipe dishes! I don't want to!"

Just that minute Mom called me to wake up and come to help her. Well, I woke up halfway at first, and I was as mad as anything, which any doctor will tell you is natural for anybody when he gets waked up without wanting to be. But my dad who is a real honest-to-goodness Christian and knows the Bible from *a* to *z* and not only *says* he is, but actually acts like one at home as well as in church, says the *Bible* says, "Be ye angry and sin not." And that means if somebody or something makes you angry, you ought to tie up your anger like you do a mad bull, and not let it run wild. Dad says a boy's temper under control is like a fire in a stove, useful for many things, but when it isn't controlled, it's like a fire in a haymow or a forest. Some people actually die many years sooner than they ought to 'cause they get mad so many times and stay mad so long it makes them sick.

Maybe my dad tells me these things especially because I'm red-haired and maybe am too quick-tempered. He says if I don't lose my temper all the time, but keep it under control, it'll help me do many important things while I'm growing up.

So, as angry as I was for being waked up, and for having to wash dishes—wipe them, I guess it was—I can hardly remember now—I tied up my anger as quick as I could. I didn't say a word or

grumble or anything. I didn't even frown. Say, do you know how many muscles of your face have to work to make a fierce-looking frown? Maybe you wouldn't believe it, but it actually takes sixty-five, our schoolteacher says, and it only takes thirteen muscles to make a smile. So it's a waste of energy to go around frowning when you're already tired and lazy.

While I was on the way from our living room to the kitchen to help Mom, I remembered something Dad had told me one day when I was going around our barnyard with a big scowl on my very freckled face. This is what he said, "Bill Collins, you're making the same face while you're a boy that you'll have to look at in the mirror all the rest of your life."

That had made me scowl deeper than ever, and I had gone away toward the barn still scowling, but not saying anything. The minute I got into the barn, though, I took out of my pocket a little round mirror which I was carrying, and looked at myself, and because I was angry I scowled and scowled and made a fierce face and stuck out my tongue at myself, and hated myself for a while. Then I saw a big, long, brown rat dart across the barn floor, and in a flash I was chasing after it and calling for our old Mixy-cat to come and do her work and to see to it that there weren't so many live rats around the Collins family's barn.

What Dad had said didn't soak in at all until

one day Mom told me almost the same thing only in different words. My grayish-brown-haired mom has the kindest face I ever saw, and her forehead is very smooth, without any deep creases in it—either going across it or running up and down in it. Just for fun one day I asked her if she'd been *ironing* it, it was so smooth, and say! Do you know what she said? She said, "I've been ironing it all my life. I've kept the frowns and wrinkles off ever since I was a little girl, so the muscles that make frowns and wrinkles won't have a chance to grow," which they will if they get too much exercise. So it would be better for even a girl to be cheerful while she's little enough to be still growing, so she'll have a face like my mom's when she gets big.

Well, I thought all those thoughts in a jiffy, even before I was halfway to the kitchen. On the way, I stepped into our downstairs bedroom for a half-jiffy to look at Charlotte Ann, who is my little one-year-old baby sister, and has pretty brownish-red curls and several small freckles on her nose. She was supposed to be sleeping and wasn't. She was lying there holding a noisy rattle in one hand and shaking it and trying to take it apart to see what made it rattle, and shouldn't have been. I stood there looking down at her pretty pink cheeks and her brownish-red hair and her chubby little fists which were all tangled up with the rattle, and at a kinda disgusted pucker

11

on her forehead 'cause the rattle wouldn't come apart.

"Listen, Charlotte Ann," I said, scowling at her, "you're making the same kind of face now you'll have to look at in the mirror all the rest of your life. You've got to think pretty thoughts if you want to have a pretty face." Then I went out into the kitchen and into the bathroom where I washed my hands with soap, which is what you're supposed to do before you wipe dishes, or else maybe Mom will have to wash the dishes over again and the drying towel too.

I still felt cranky, but I kept thinking about the airplane trip the gang was going to take to Chicago—all the gang except me, so far, and so I kept my fire in the stove. I knew that pretty soon my parents would have to decide something, so I kept on hoping it would be "Yes."

My mom had been teaching me to sing tenor, and sometimes on Sunday nights, when she'd play the organ in our front room, she and Dad and I would sing trios, which helped to make us all like each other better. So while we were doing dishes that noon, Mom and I started singing different songs, which were the ones we used in school and also some of the gospel songs we used in church, and the next thing we knew, the dishes were done and set away, and in a jiffy I was free to go and pick beans if I wanted to, or if I didn't want to. I was wishing I could run

lickety-sizzle out across our yard through the gate and across the dusty graveled road, vault over the rail fence on the other side and fly down the path through the woods, down the hill past the big birch tree to the spring where the gang was supposed to meet at two o'clock, if they could. Sometimes we couldn't because most of us had to work some of the time. Today was one of the days I couldn't.

As soon as I'd finished wiping the last dish, which was our big long platter that had had the fried chicken on it, I went back into our bathroom and washed my hands again, which Mom had taught me to do. While I was rinsing them, I looked past my ordinary-looking face and saw my dad's reflection in the mirror. He was standing outside our bathroom window, which was closed tight to keep out some of the terrific heat that was outdoors. Standing right beside him was Old Man Paddler.

For those of you who've never heard of Old Man Paddler, I'd better say that he's the best friend the Sugar Creek Gang ever had or ever will have. He lives up in the hills above Sugar Creek and likes boys and he has put us all into his will, which he says he's already made. Well, he and my dad were standing there talking, and the old man's gnarled old hands were gesturing around in a sort of circle and he was moving them up and down, and pointing toward the sky. Right

away I guessed he was talking about the airplane trip to Chicago. I could see his long, white whiskers bobbing up and down like a man's whiskers do when he's talking. All of a sudden, he and Dad reached out and shook hands with each other and then started walking toward the house.

Say! All of another sudden a great thrill came running and jumped right kersmack into the middle of my heart and I was so happy it began to hurt inside terribly, 'cause you know what? I *knew* that I was going to get to go with the rest of the gang. The reason was just that minute, while Dad was opening the screen door to our kitchen to let Old Man Paddler in first, Dad said, "All right, we'll let him go!"

My hands weren't even dry when I left that bathroom. In fact, I didn't even see the towel that slipped from the rack where I'd tossed it up in too big a hurry, and it fell on the floor. I wanted to make a dive for that old man's whiskers and hug him. Instead, I just stood there trembling and looking, seeing myself sailing along through the air with big white clouds all around our airplane, and the earth away down below me. I even felt like I had wings.

Pretty soon, we were all in our living room where it was cooler than in the kitchen, and we were all sitting down in different chairs, I having my bare feet twisted around and underneath my chair and fastened onto the rounds, and was rock-

ing back and forth, noticing that with every rock the chair crept sidewise a little over the rug toward Charlotte Ann's bassinet, which Mom had just brought in.

It was kinda like a meeting of some sort at first, with all of us sitting quiet, then Dad cleared his big voice and said, "Well, Bill, Mr. Paddler has persuaded me to let him invest a little money in you. He wants to pay your way to Chicago by airplane. His nephew, Barry Boyland, has agreed to come and be chaperone to the whole Sugar Creek Gang." There was a twinkle in the old man's eyes, and several of them in Dad's and also some in Mom's, as Dad finished by saying the beans could be picked later in the day when it was cooler, and that I really ought to meet with the gang today, if I wanted to, and—

Say, just as quick as I could, after I'd courteously thanked the kind, old trembling-voiced man, I was out of our house, running through the heat waves, toward our front gate. I frisked across the graveled road, stirring up a lot of dust, vaulted over the rail fence and went like greased lightning toward the spring, imagining myself to be an airplane and trying to make a noise like one, wishing I was one, and almost bursting to tell the news to the rest of the gang.

My dad's last words were ringing in my ears too, as I flew through the woods, with my voice droning like an airplane. This is what he said,

while we were still in the parlor, "Of course, Bill, we shall expect you to keep your eyes open and learn a lot of things while you're there. Make it an educational trip as well as a pleasure trip."

My own answer was very quick. "Sure," I said, and was already halfway across the room to the door. I remembered my promise though, later, and kept it too, when I wrote a letter to my parents from Chicago.

ZZZZZZ-RRRRRR! On my way to the spring!

2

THE MINUTE I got to the top of the hill which is just above the spring where our gang nearly always meets, I looked down ahead of me and saw nearly all the gang there, sprawled on the long, mashed-down green and brown grass, each one lying in a different direction. As usual Circus was sitting perched on a limb of a tree chattering like a monkey, getting ready to do an acrobatic stunt of some kind.

I dashed past the old beech tree which has all our initials carved on its smooth, gray bark, and in a jiffy, after turning a somersault, was lying down beside everybody, panting and trying to get myself to stop breathing so hard. I tell you it felt good to know I had good news for them, and it felt good to be with the gang again, after I'd been thinking all day that I'd have to pick beans instead of being allowed to go in swimming.

Good old Gang! I thought, still panting. There was Poetry, the barrel-shaped member of the gang, who has maybe the keenest mind of all of us, especially when it comes to arithmetic. We had

17

named him Poetry 'cause he knows so many different poems, and any minute something might remind him of one, and we'd either have to listen to it or else shush him up, if we could. He was my very best friend most of the time. He and Circus were always in a good-natured argument with each other. In fact, they were in one that very minute. Circus called down from the limb of the tree where he was and said, "Say, Poetry, do you know why I like you?"

"Why?" Poetry's squawky voice called back up to him.

" 'Cause," Circus called back down, " 'cause, in the winter I can use you for a windbreak to keep the cold wind off, and in the summertime I can lie down behind you in the shade to keep cool."

It was a very old joke, but we laughed anyway. Circus came sliding down out of his tree right that minute, to lie down kersmack beside Poetry on the shady side of him, which started a good-natured fight.

Well, I told the gang the crazy dream I'd had about the doctor, which was myself, giving a blood transfusion with raspberry juice, and that reminded Big Jim that one time before he'd moved into Sugar Creek territory, he had had to have a blood transfusion himself, because he had been hurt in a mowing machine. He rolled up his right trouser leg to show us a big, long, white scar,

with a lot of stitch scars from one end of it to the other, making it look like a long, white worm with eight pairs of legs. We'd seen the scar before, but I just never told you about it.

Then Big Jim rolled over and sat up and grinned and said, "I have a very special kind of blood, which is called type B. Not more than seven people in a hundred have it. They had a hard time finding anybody to give me his blood, and I almost died."

Of course I was interested in that, since I was going to be a doctor. We all let him tell his story over again, even though we'd heard it a good many times. Then we talked about what we'd like to see when we got to Chicago. Little Jim said he wanted to visit the zoo to see if maybe his pet bear was there. He'd had one once, you know, and had had to sell it to some zoo when it got too big and too cross to be a pet.

When he mentioned the bear, I looked over at him and there were tears in his eyes, 'cause he'd really liked that little cub very much. Say! That brave little guy had saved all our lives once when he'd shot the cub's fierce old mother bear when she was so mad she could have killed all of us.

I'd better not get started on that story, though, but you can have somebody tell you about it who has read it in a book called *We Killed a Bear*. Boy, oh boy, the way Little Jim grabbed that rifle and rammed it down that old mother bear's

19

old savage old red throat with her big teeth looking like an alligator's! But this story is about the Sugar Creek Gang in Chicago, so I can't get off on that exciting bear's tale now. Also, Little Jim said, he wanted to go to one of the big department stores when we got to Chicago and ride up and down on an escalator.

Big Jim wanted to see the Federal Reserve Bank, 'cause he's interested in business and wants to be a banker sometime. Big Jim is the oldest member of our gang, has fuzz on his upper lip most of the time, was once a Boy Scout and has the best manners of any boy his age. He is always especially courteous to Sylvia, our minister's oldest daughter, and can lick the stuffin's out of any boy his age. He still has a scar on one of the knuckles of his right hand where the skin was split open on a bank robber's jaw once. Say, *that* was some experience! The Sugar Creek Gang captured that robber in the middle of the night saving Old Man Paddler's life, which if we hadn't we wouldn't have had our free airplane trip to Chicago. That's another thing I found out. The old man was going to pay *all* our fares himself, and also pay his nephew, Barry Boyland, a salary while he was being our chaperone. Barry, you know, was the big, brown-faced, grand young man who took us on our camping trip up north.

Well, there we were, lying there in the grass just above the spring, talking, laughing, doing

stunts, each one trying to say something funnier than the other one. Big Jim, Little Jim, Circus, Dragonfly, Poetry and—oh yes, Tom Till. Little Tom's parents were poor, mostly because his dad spent most of his money for whiskey. Little Tom is the new member of our gang and has red hair and can't help it. For a minute, while we were lying there I looked over at his nose and noticed that it was nice and straight where I'd once smashed it in a fight and it looked like any boy's nose ought to. Poor little Tom's dad is always bragging about how he can take a drink of whiskey or else leave it alone, whichever he wants to. Dad says every sad old man in the world who is a drunkard now, used to brag about how he could take a drink or else leave it alone, when he wanted to. Maybe I'd better say that Little Tom's big brother Bob had been licked good and hard once in a fight with Big Jim, and that he hated Big Jim terribly, and might do most anything to get even with him.

And while I'm telling you about drunkards, I ought to tell you that Circus' dad used to be one, but he's what the Bible calls "born again" now, and his money goes into clothes and food and shoes for his family instead of into his stomach, which is getting well again after having ulcers.

And that's all the Sugar Creek Gang except me, Bill Collins, whose real and full name is William Jasper Collins, a name which I don't like, and

which my parents call me sometimes when I haven't been behaving myself very well. I'd actually rather be good than to have them call me that.

We were lying there, each one of us chewing on the ends of different pieces of grass, like boys do, and for a minute I was thinking of how cows sometimes lie down like that and chew the grass they've already eaten, swallowing backward to bring it up into their mouths. Then, when they've chewed it all they want to, they swallow it down into their other stomach and manufacture it into milk. Just as I was thinking of how our little Charlotte Ann was getting big enough to stop drinking milk out of a bottle and to drink it like a human being, I heard a noise up the creek. It sounded like a lot of boys in swimming in our own swimming hole. Big Jim jerked his head up real quick, making me think for a minute, not of a cow, but of a general in an army. If there was anything our gang didn't like, it was for an outside gang of boys to come into Sugar Creek territory and act like they owned the place. That's why we'd had the fierce battle of Bumblebee Hill the summer before, when Bob and his gang of rough town boys had come out and eaten up our strawberries. That was the time Big Jim had licked big Bob Till for the first time Bob had ever been licked, and also the time when I'd smashed little red-haired Tom's nose, and all the rest of us had licked all the rest of *them*.

So, while I was lying there, sprawled out like a small cow, listening to the hollering up the creek, my fists began to double up, and my temper started to get hot. I could see the rest of the gang was feeling the same way. There really wasn't anything very selfish about our gang, and we wouldn't have cared very much if other people used our swimming hole, if they'd be careful not to spoil it; but the last time Bob's gang had been there they'd broken down two or three pretty little ash saplings on which we usually hung our clothes, and they'd turned our diving raft upside down and left it with mud smeared all over the top.

Just that minute I rolled over in the grass, bumping into Poetry and getting stopped like I had bumped into a stone wall, just at the very moment Dragonfly, who as I told you is always seeing things first, said, "Look! There's our diving raft floating downstream!"

And sure enough it was. Upside down and floating downstream, right toward where we were. In fact it looked like it would bump into the bank right in front of the spring.

Well, that was too much. It looked like there was going to be another famous battle.

We scrambled to our feet. That is, we started to, but Big Jim stopped us, by saying, "Sh! Lie

down. *All* of you. Keep still! Wait till I see what the note says.''

What note? I thought. Then I saw a piece of paper lying on top of the raft, and a big rock lying on top of it to hold it down, so the wind wouldn't blow it off.

In about a jiffy, with the rest of us keeping still and lying where we were, Big Jim stood up with a grim face and walked over to the spring and down the little steep bank to the edge of the creek. He made us lie still or we wouldn't have, 'cause that raft upside down was like a red flag being waved in front of seven mad bulls which weren't tied.

I looked over the top of Poetry's fat side to Little Jim, and he was holding onto his stick, which he nearly always carried, very tight, so tight that his knuckles were white.

In a flash Big Jim had his clothes off and was swimming and wading out toward the raft. In another flash, he was dragging the raft after him toward our shore, while we lay there like the springs in a bunch of jack-in-the-boxes, waiting for somebody to press the button.

''Look!'' Dragonfly hissed to us. ''See where they cut the ropes! Our *new ropes!*'' I was already seeing it. They'd cut the ropes which we'd put on the raft to anchor it to the bottom.

Big Jim used one of the ropes to tie the raft to the root of a tree that grew there on the bank of

the creek, then he lifted the rock off the piece of paper, and without even stopping to dress, 'cause he wasn't dry yet anyway, he picked up his clothes and came back to where we were. I could see the big muscles on his arms, especially the ones between his shoulders and his elbows which are called the biceps muscles, and I thought how much bigger they were than mine, and also how hard they were when he tensed them. Our gang was always showing each other our biceps, and looking proud 'cause each week they seemed a little bit bigger and harder, but weren't.

Well, Big Jim handed the note to Poetry, who sat up and read it, his squawky voice sounding more than ever like a duck with a bad cold, and also like he was having a chill. His hand was shaking a little too, while he held it, and this is what he read:

> To the Sugar Creek Gang:
> Gentlemen and cowards! A swimming hole is no place for a choir platform. Anyway we can't use it, so we're shipping it down to you, express collect. If you don't like it, you can lump it!

Well, the minute Poetry finished reading the note out loud, we were all ready to fight. It was an insult. Maybe you know that the Sugar Creek Gang all went to church every Sunday and weren't

ashamed of it. In fact anybody in the world that wants to amount to a hill of soup beans ought to go to church.

"It's an *insult!*" Poetry squawked. "Let's go up there and lick the stuffin's out of them!" By that time we were all rolled over on our stomachs and were waiting for orders from Big Jim.

"Read the signature," Poetry said and passed it to Big Jim. Big Jim looked at it and we all squirmed around and read it over his shoulders, and this is what it said:

> Yours truly,
> THE HELLFIRE GANG

The silly bunch of copycats! I thought, and remembered that my dad had told me once that over a hundred years ago, when a famous Presbyterian evangelist was preaching in a town, there was a wild gang of boys there who had called themselves The Hellfire Club. Anyway, maybe you know that Bob Till's dad was an atheist, and Bob and little red-haired Tom had never been to Sunday school in their lives until I had got Tom to start going with the Collins family, and he had finally joined our gang.

The next thing I knew, Big Jim had folded the paper and tucked it into one of the pockets of his overalls, which, right that minute, he was starting to pull on. He did it very slowly, as if he was

26

thinking. His jaw was set hard and his lips were pressed together in a straight line, which meant plenty. But say! When he got through dressing, he plunked himself down on the grass again and with his fists still doubled up, stared out across the woods toward a stump where I saw a little reddish-brown chipmunk sitting straight up, holding an acorn or something in its forepaws and eating very, very fast like chipmunks do. Then Big Jim rolled over and lay down in the sun.

"What?" I thought. "Are we going to lie here like a bunch of saps and let the Hellfire Gang spoil our swimming hole?" Then I looked over the top of Dragonfly's head and saw Little Tom Till's messed-up red hair, and his five or six hundred freckles and his very pretty blue eyes which looked kinda like there was a sad fire in them, and I knew there wasn't going to be any fight, and why. Big Jim simply wouldn't lead the gang into battle under such circumstances.

It's a terrible letdown, though, to be all keyed up to have a good fight, and then not get to have it, especially when you know the other gang needs a licking. I remembered what a grand fight our other one had been, when Big Jim had led us to victory. Remember the way he did it? How he stepped out from the bushes where he had been lying in ambush, and walked stiff-legged, like a dog does when it walks out toward a new dog it's never seen before? How Big Jim stepped out and

looked up to the top of the hill where Bob and his gang were calling us all kinds of names? How Big Jim stood there, and said, "Fellows, it isn't a question of whether we're afraid to fight. There isn't a man among us that's got a drop of coward's blood in him!"

We still didn't have any of that kind of blood, but we didn't dare fight with Little Tom belonging to our gang, and his brother Bob belonging to the other. It wouldn't be fair to Tom.

And now, let's get started to Chicago. I've had to tell you about this almost-fight, so you'll understand what happened in Chicago, when Big Jim and Bob met again under the strangest circumstances you ever saw. Of course none of us knew that Bob would be there in Chicago ahead of us, and certainly none of us ever dreamed *why* he'd be there, but he was.

3

It WAS THE MORNING BEFORE we were to leave
for Chicago, when I found out that Bob Till had
gone there ahead of us, and why. Mom and Dad
and I were sitting at our breakfast table, each one
of us having finished eating. Charlotte Ann was
in her bassinet in the other room. Dad reached
over to a corner of the table for our Bible which
was always on that corner at mealtime. All of us
knew that we would have what we called "family devotions" at our house at least once a day,
and we usually had it at the table. Sometimes
Dad would read, sometimes Mom, and sometimes me. Once in a while, we just passed around
what is called a "Bread Box" which is a little
square box full of Bible verses printed on little
cards.

Dad reached for the Bible, and I sat quiet,
listening, 'cause even though I was anxious to
get outdoors and feel the bare ground under my
bare feet, and even though Johnny Wren was
outside on our clothesline just whooping it up
with his song which sounded like a lot of beauti-

ful jibberish all mixed up with different tones, I knew the Bible was the most important book in the world, and I was supposed to listen respectfully. Little Jim's mom had taught him—and he had told me—that it was full of sweet music.

Well, Dad opened the Bible respectfully, and asked me to read, which I started to do, when there was a knock on our screen door. We were eating breakfast that morning in our kitchen, so the door wasn't very far behind me. I turned around and looked, and there, kinda half-sitting and half-standing on the steps, was little Tom Till, the only Christian in the whole Till family, looking very sad, like something had happened to him. His hook-nosed dad was always giving him a licking without finding out first whether he needed it or not, I thought.

"Come in, Tom," Mom said, going to the screen door and opening it, and Little Tom bashfully came in and looked around at the different things in the kitchen, such as our new refrigerator and a gas stove which we used especially in the summer so Mom wouldn't half smother to death getting meals for the Collins family.

"We're having family altar," I said to Little Tom Till. Dad reached behind him for a chair and Little Tom sat down between him and me. Just that minute Charlotte Ann started a funny cooing noise in the other room in her bassinet which she nearly always does when she wakes up

in the morning, just like birds do, but she wasn't
crying, so Mom didn't go to get her. Charlotte
Ann always half-sang and half-gurgled in the
morning when she was feeling good, which she
nearly always was.

I knew Tom Till didn't know what family altar
was, which most boys in the world don't because
their parents are not like mine, and maybe don't
know God well enough to talk to Him.

Pretty soon I was reading the passage Dad had
picked out, and it was about people giving their
bodies to God, so He could use them to do what
needed to be done in the world. Just like a great
musician playing on a violin or a piano, so we
were supposed to let God play on *us*, or else use
us like a carpenter uses his tools to build something.

Little Tom Till's and my red hair were so close
together and only a little different in color that
for a minute I let my mind stray to a pretty
two-tone automobile which Dad had bought just
the other day. Mom had a notebook in her hand
and she wrote down one of the best verses I'd
read. She did that at every family altar meeting
we had, and then once every week, or whenever
we wanted to, we checked back over the verses
we'd talked about and recalled the different things
they meant.

Dad explained to Tom why we did that, saying,
"A boy who goes to Sunday school every Sunday for a year, still only gets about twenty-six

31

hours a year Bible instruction, and that isn't very much, out of eight thousand seven hundred sixty hours in a year.''

It didn't take us very long, but when we got through, I understood what the verses meant. If God had my whole body, including my mind, hands, feet, eyes, ears and all of me, I'd be a grand little guy, which I really wasn't most of the time.

If He had my eyes, I oughtn't to look at things I oughtn't to; if he had my feet, I wouldn't let them carry me places I oughtn't go; if He had my ears I wouldn't listen to the tough boy's filthy talk at school; and if He had my tongue I'd tell them in no uncertain terms that their words sounded like the mud in our barnyard looked. And I wouldn't fuss or whine when my parents told me to do something my lazy body didn't want to do; and I'd be polite and wouldn't talk back to my parents, even when I thought maybe they might have made a mistake in something they accused me of doing and I hadn't done it.

I never saw anybody look so interested and also like he was all stirred up inside, as Little Tom Till. When we'd finished saying things about the verses I'd read, and Mom had finished writing them down, one of them especially, Dad started in to sing the chorus of a church hymn, and I joined in with a kind of tenor and Mom with an alto. Tom didn't know the song at all,

and didn't have much of a voice for singing anyway, so he just listened.

We finished the chorus and Dad got ready to pray. "Are there any requests?" he asked, like he nearly always does.

"Pray for Old Man Paddler," I said, "he doesn't feel very well."

"Pray for our minister," Mom said, and I thought right away of Sylvia our new minister's oldest daughter whom Big Jim seems to kinda like better than anybody. Then my mind flashed to Circus' kinda ordinary-looking sister who wasn't saved yet, who I'd tried to kill a spider for last year at school and didn't because of her thinking I was afraid of it and killing it herself. And even though I don't like girls and I especially didn't like her, I thought she ought to be saved, anyway, so I said, "Pray for—" And then I felt the roots of my hair acting like they were worms and were all starting to crawl at once. I knew that if I had been looking at my freckled face in the mirror, I'd be blushing like a silly person.

Dad looked at me a jiffy, and I bowed my head and shut my eyes and shut up, and he said to Tom, "Any request? Anything or anybody you want us to pray for?"

I'd forgotten Tom for a minute, so I opened my eyes again and I saw him swallow like he'd forgotten to chew a big bite of something, and

then he said, "Pray for B-bob, he's—he ran away this morning—"

Dad prayed only a very few minutes, and in language we could all understand. Then at the end of his prayer, he prayed for all our gang by name, especially for Big Bob Till, who it seemed he already knew about. I thought it was kinda funny that he prayed for Mr. Simondson, our grocer, right along with Bob, and it wasn't until afterward that I found out that Bob Till had broken into his store last night and stolen money out of the cash register.

After breakfast, when Tom and I were outdoors getting ready to dig potatoes which he had come over to our house especially to help me do that day, my Mom having hired him on purpose so he would have a little spending money when he got to Chicago, I asked him where Bob had gone.

"I don't know," he said, digging one of his bare toes into the soft dirt of our garden. "Maybe he went to Chicago. He's been a-wantin' to go there for a long time."

"Chicago?" I said, and he said, "Sh! Not so loud. And please don't tell anybody, or the police'll get him."

I felt sorry for little Tom, and I knew if he'd had parents like mine or like most of the boys in our gang had, Bob would have been different and would have had Bible verses growing in his heart

34

and mind instead of a lot of big ugly sins, like the tall ugly weeds that grew on both sides of the path on the way to our potato patch.

There wouldn't have been any big weeds there, I thought, if I'd pulled them up or cut them down when they were little.

Anyway, I got to wondering what if when we got to Chicago, we found Bob Till there somewhere, and I wished we would. In fact I kinda *knew* we would.

Tom and I worked hard, digging potatoes, until ten o'clock, when Mom called us to come in and have a cup of chocolate milk, my mom doing it more for Tom's sake than for mine, I having enough vitamins in my diet, but Tom's eyes always looked like he needed more food of some kind. We dropped our potato forks and walked back to the house. When we got to the lawn, we started stepping on the different gray dandelion heads, doing it all the way to our back door, looking like we were football players trying to dodge somebody on the other team. I was always doing that in our kitchen too, walking around and stepping on my favorite patterns on the linoleum, until Mom's nerves couldn't stand it any longer, and then I'd go outdoors awhile.

I didn't even tell Mom or Dad what Tom had

told me about Bob. That day finally passed by, with the thing in my mind almost all the time: *"Big Bob Till is in Chicago. Big Bob Till is in Chicago where the Sugar Creek Gang is going."*

At last the next day came. I was up early and acting almost like a chicken with its head cut off. Dad and Poetry's dad drove us all to the nearest big city where there was an airport. We drove right down through the center of town, and it seemed like everybody turned to look at us—or else at Dad's new two-tone automobile. Old Man Paddler was sitting in the front seat with him. "I wish I were young enough to learn to drive," that kind old man said, his whiskers bobbing.

Pretty soon we were at the airport, and inside the station where Barry Boyland, the old man's nephew, was getting our tickets, and where our baggage was being checked for weight, each one of us being allowed to take not more than forty pounds of luggage.

It was almost like an ordinary railroad station, with opera chairs all around the wall. There was a soda fountain on one end and a place to buy your favorite kind of pop.

Well, on the other side of the ticket window was a control room with two men who had earphones on their heads, listening and talking like people do who are technicians in an airport.

All of us were sitting beside each other in a long row, with Little Jim on one side of me and

Poetry on the other. I'd been reading up on air-planes almost all summer—anyway, after we knew we were going to ride in one—so I explained nearly everything to Little Jim, while we were waiting for our plane to come.

"What are those men doing over there?" Little Jim asked, motioning toward the technicians.

"They're probably talking to the pilots up in some airplane," I said, and Big Jim finished explaining it by saying, "They're using a radio telephone to tell them about weather conditions."

Weather conditions, you know, are very important for airplane officers to know about. I was glad it was a sunny day with only scattered clouds, although I knew a day could start like that at Sugar Creek, and before the afternoon came, there could be a terrific thunderstorm, and I wished there wouldn't be one while we were right up there in the middle of where they came from.

Say, I couldn't any more stay sat down than anything, and neither could the rest of us. As soon as they would let us, we went through the gate outside, and stood just outside the heavy woven-wire fence to watch the baggage and mail trucks moving around and to look at the different people and to wait.

Away off to the right was an airplane hangar where there were a lot of little airplanes going up and coming down all the time, maybe taking up

passengers, or else teaching young pilots to fly or something.

All of a sudden there was a mighty roaring in the sky and we saw our plane circling, getting ready to come down. Boy, oh boy! I was tingling inside, half scared to death. Say, that big plane actually looked like a great big long round house with a lot of windows, with two great big wings spread out like an eagle's, and it looked fierce as it sailed right down to the ground and came taxiing along the runway straight toward the airport. Bigger and bigger, longer and longer, with the propellers of its two engines whirling around like two big windmills. It stopped right in front of us.

Somebody pushed a little stairway on wheels up to the plane, a door opened in the side and some smiling, important-looking people came tripping down the portable stairway and walked toward the station. The plane had ten minutes to stay, so the people could get off and stretch and look arond if they wanted to.

Somebody pushed a hand truck up to the mail and baggage compartments which were in the plane's long nose, just between its two eyes, which were the propellers and which weren't turning now.

Poetry and I were standing beside the gate, watching the people coming off the plane, and the pilot and the copilot, and the stewardess, who

was smiling and wearing dark glasses and light shoes and a brownish suit like Little Jim's mom wears sometimes. The stewardess and the two pilots are what is called the flight crew.

Well, that ten minutes dragged past like a snail, and pretty soon it was time to get on ourselves. Our tickets had been ordered ahead of time, or else we couldn't have gone, 'cause in these days more and more people are traveling by air and you have to have reservations.

"Well, here goes," I thought, and Poetry, who was right behind me, started to quote from John Adams' famous speech: "Sink or swim, live or die, survive or perish, I give my heart and hand to this vote. . . ." From that he swung off into a gospel chorus which was popular in our junior meeting in church, which goes:

Here I go in my airplane, up in the air so high,
  High in my gospel airplane, far up into the sky,
Leaving the world so far below, as higher and
      higher I go,
    You are invited to go with me, up in my air-
      plane.

The second verse starts like this: "Yes, I'll go in your airplane, up in the air so high." Then it ends with the words "I am delighted to go with you, up in your airplane."

Poetry didn't get to finish the poem which he

39

was actually trying to *sing* on the way up the portable stairway and into the plane.

"Heart, get out of my mouth!" I felt like saying, 'cause it felt like it was there. At the top of the little stairs, and just inside the plane, on the right, was a little door leading into a room of some kind, which I afterward learned was a lavatory with running water and everything.

Say, it was just like a train inside, with a row of seats on each side of a narrow aisle, nice soft, cushioned seats like the ones in our new car, with a window beside each one. I followed Poetry up the narrow aisle to where they wanted me to sit. I say, "up," 'cause the airplane was parked, you know, and the tail when the plane is parked is lower than the nose, so we had to climb up a little hill inside to get to our seats. The ceiling was actually almost a foot higher than my head, the plane was that big.

Pretty soon we were all there, with Poetry in front of me, Dragonfly behind me and Little Jim right across the aisle. The rest of us were on one side or the other.

Pretty soon after that the flight crew came in, the door was shut and locked and we were ready. I looked out my little window to watch somebody pushing the portable stairway away, and to look at the people who were waving good-bye to us. And there, standing just inside the gate and beside my dad, was Old Man Paddler, looking like

one of the pictures I'd seen once of a man named Potatoe Creek Johnny who lived out west in the Black Hills and had discovered the largest gold nugget ever found there. His long white whiskers hung clear down his chest, almost to his belt. He had a cane in his right hand which he had to use that summer, because he was getting older and older and couldn't walk so well. I looked at my dad's big blackish-red eyebrows and at his moustache and at Dad himself, and swallowed something that was stuck in my throat. Then the big motors started to turn, first one and then the other, and in a jiffy the plane itself began to move. The first thing it did was to turn clear around and move slowly off on its three big balloon tires, two in front just below the place where the wings were fastened onto its body, and the other away back under the end of the tail. I couldn't see them from where I was but I'd noticed them when I was outside.

I forgot to say that the stewardess came through first, before we started, and showed us how to fasten on our safety belts and gave us some gum to chew. We were supposed to chew gum, so that when we got up in the air it would help our ears to keep from feeling like they had dwarfs in them, pounding with little hammers and trying to get out.

Pretty soon our plane came to a runway, and turned left and moved faster and faster on the

runway out across the field to the farther end, and I expected any minute to start going up into the air. Boy, I held on to the sides of my seat, I can tell you. But we didn't go up. Instead, when we got to the other side of the field, we stopped, and the plane turned halfway around until we were crossways on the runway. All of a sudden the motors started to roar, first one and then the other and the propellers went faster than a humming-bird's wings do.

"Wh-what's that for?" Dragonfly asked me, his eyes bulging a little. "What's the matter? Won't it go up?"

It certainly wasn't doing anything but standing still, like an automobile standing crossways with the road, and with the motors roaring. But Po-etry, who had been studying airplanes even more than I had, knew what was going on, so he called back to Dragonfly and said, "They've quartered it into the wind, and they're testing the motors to see if they're all right. You wouldn't want anything to go wrong with them up in the sky, would you?"

Little Jim heard him say that, and for a minute he looked scared but he was grinning and even though his hands were holding onto the arms of his chair so tight the knuckles were white, I knew he wouldn't let being scared keep him from en-joying the ride.

"What's *quartered into the wind* mean?" Drag-onfly wanted to know.

"Dividing it into four equal parts," Poetry said with a sober face.

Dragonfly's eyebrow went down. He didn't feel like joking, so Poetry explained it, and Dragonfly was satisfied.

Well, the motors must have been all right, for pretty soon the plane turned the rest of the way around and we started to move, straight against the wind, faster and faster, and in a jiffy the tail began to rise up and we were all sitting level. Faster and faster, and faster and faster, and looking out, I saw that we weren't on the ground any more but were climbing.

4

Say, it didn't even seem like we were in an airplane, anyway not like I thought it would seem. There wasn't any sensation of being high, which a person has when he is standing on a high cliff looking down, or when he is up in a high tree along Sugar Creek and the wind is blowing the tree back and forth; and that was because of our not having any contact with the earth. Poetry, and the book I'd been reading, said that was the reason, anyway. It was just like we were in a big, long automobile, which was riding on an air road which you couldn't see. Even the big, noisy motors seemed quiet, 'cause the plane was kinda soundproof.

It surely was fun. As soon as we got over the first thrill, we began to look down toward where the people of the earth lived and to mention different things we could see.

"We're going right straight toward Sugar Creek," I heard Circus say. I looked across at him and he had on his monkey face. He'd rather be up high in the air than any place else, that

maybe being the reason why he was always climbing a tree or a barn or something. Anyway, maybe that was why, when he practiced the songs he was going to sing in the Chicago church and over the radio, he nearly always climbed up in a tree to do it.

I sat there, feeling the safety belt across my stomach, just above my lap, and for a minute, looking inside and up to the front, I saw the little chrome-colored door which was closed, and on the other side of which, I knew, were two expert pilots who had received what is called basic instruction in the United States Army, or maybe in the Navy or Marine Corps, and that they were in good health, each one having to pass a rigid physical examination every six months, like all pilots do who drive planes with passengers in them. I knew that the copilot could run the plane just as well as the pilot could, 'cause he'd had the same training, and if anything should happen to the pilot, he could run it himself. They were sitting side by side like two people do who sit in the front seat of an automobile. I knew that, because I'd seen them, just before they had shut the door.

Say, it didn't take us only several jiffies before we were riding over the hills above Sugar Creek, only it seemed we weren't even moving, we were so high, and the hills looked like little anthills.

"Look!" Dragonfly exclaimed, "There's Old

Man Paddler's cabin!'' which it wasn't, but was a great big creamery where my dad sold our cream, and was ten times as big as Old Man Paddler's house with its clapboard roof.

"And there's Sugar Creek itself,'' Little Tom Till said. It was, all right, only it looked like a little twisted, crooked silver thread. I tried to see where the swimming hole was, but couldn't. I did see Bumblebee Hill though, where we'd licked the stuffin's out of that gang of rough boys the summer before.

In another second, it seemed, 'cause we were moving at the rate of four hundred miles an hour, although it seemed like only about twenty, we were up so high, we were over our town. Dragonfly, like he nearly always does, saw something that wasn't what he thought it was.

"See *there!*'' he exclaimed again. I guess we nearly all forgot there were other passengers in the plane, even though we were being very quiet for a bunch of ordinarily noisy boys.

"What?'' Poetry said.

"There's my mother down there waving one of Dad's big colored handkerchiefs at me.''

"You're crazy,'' Poetry said. "That's the American flag on the top of the flagpole,'' which most of us agreed it was.

And then Sugar Creek was gone and we were on our way to Chicago.

Each one of us, I noticed, had a little ice

cream container right beside our seat, which was empty and would hold about a pint. Dragonfly hadn't noticed his yet, and when he did, he asked what was it for. Poetry explained by saying, "That's where you put your breakfast in case for any reason you decide you don't want it any longer."

You should have seen Dragonfly's look. Looking at him made me feel like he looked, and I could tell that he was beginning to be tired of his breakfast already. Maybe everything would have been all right if Poetry hadn't been reminded of a story of a little boy who had gone to a Sunday school picnic and had eaten too much ice cream. Anyway, Poetry told the story, which was about a boy who looked very sad, after eating maybe seven double-dip ice cream cones.

"What's the matter?" his teacher asked him. "Didn't you get all you wanted?" And the little fellow looked sadder still and held his stomach and said, "I—I—I don't w-w-want a-all I g-got."

I could see that that didn't help Dragonfly any, for he began to look just a little pale and I knew pretty soon he might have what is called "altitude sickness" which hardly ever happens to a person in an airplane, but people on trains or in cars sometimes do get it and once in a while in an airplane, that being the reason why they have empty ice cream containers beside everybody hidden away down out of sight.

47

*   *   *

Even at that Dragonfly might not have had any trouble if the plane hadn't had to make a quick climb to higher altitude. I remembered afterward that there had been a lot of static in the control room back at the airport, which meant that not too far away there was probably an electric storm.

Well, as I told you, there had been only scattered clouds in the sky when we started, which were what is called cumulous clouds, or the kind that look like the big white bundles of wool which my dad gets from our sheep when we shear them in the spring. Some of them were below us and some above us, which meant we were flying about four thousand feet high. Barry Boyland had told us that, having studied clouds and knowing them like our gang knew different kinds of shells.

No sooner had Poetry finished his story about the Sunday school boy who didn't want all the ice cream he'd had, than the pretty stewardess in the brown suit and white shoes came walking up the soft green-rugged aisle to tell us to fasten our safety belts again, or to help us, whichever we needed, some of us having taken them off like people do after they get up and are cruising.

Very quietly, she announced, in her very businesslike but kind voice, "We're going to climb several thousand feet, to get above the storm."

48

"What storm?" I thought, 'cause I couldn't see anything but the bluest blue sky I'd ever seen, and the whitest white clouds. Of course I couldn't see straight ahead of us like the pilots could, who had windows in front of them and all around them, except straight behind.

Barry explained it to us, while we were getting our belts fastened again, and most of us were beginning to hold onto our chair arms. Barry said, "The cold air of a storm is probably coming right straight toward us in a head-on collision against the warm air which we've been flying in, and that'll form what is called a storm collar and there will be a fierce updraft that will force those beautiful cumulous clouds upward and pack them together as tight as sardines in a can and they'll be forced upward into what is called a 'thunderhead.' The pilots have probably been warned from a ground station somewhere, and they are going to climb over the thunderhead."

I wasn't scared, 'cause Barry explained it so quietly and acted like it wouldn't be any more than climbing one of the hills of Sugar Creek in an automobile. Then he yawned and stretched a little and started to read a magazine he had with him, which was a real Christian magazine. Nearly all our parents in Sugar Creek were subscribers to it, except Dragonfly's, being good readers, especially of that kind of literature.

Already I could tell we were beginning to

climb rather fast, for my ears began to pound and to feel crazy. I chewed my gum faster and swallowed and swallowed and swallowed, and my ears kept on feeling like there was a dwarf in each one pounding with a rubber mallet and trying to get the doors open so they could get out, or else they were trying to get in, I couldn't tell which.

Then I looked at Dragonfly, and he was very pale and was leaning over, looking pitifully at the still-empty ice cream container, which he already held in his right hand.

5

THERE ISN'T ANY REASON why I should take
time to tell what happened to Dragonfly after
that, 'cause if I don't hurry up, I won't get to tell
you what happened in Chicago. There was a
storm, though, right after Dragonfly lost his
breakfast.

We all thought he'd be all right after that, but
he wasn't. He kept staying pale and he was so
dizzy he couldn't sit up, which is the same as
having vertigo, a kind of swimming of the head.
We were so high, I guess we had actually climbed
to over twenty thousand feet high, and that's
pretty high, especially if you have to get there
quick, which we did. I was busy myself, chewing gum and swallowing. I hardly noticed the
stewardess coming to Dragonfly as soon as she
could with what is called a portable oxygen appa-
ratus of some sort, which had something that
could be put on over his nose like a gas mask
they use in wars, and he could breathe in all the
extra oxygen he needed. He actually acted like he
had the asthma. I'd seen my city cousin have it

once and it isn't funny to look at. He was actually blue in the face for a while.

But it didn't take us long to get over the thunderhead and down lower again, and that, with the oxygen Dragonfly was getting artificially, tided him over, and he was all right again. The funny thing was, though, after we got down lower, and were cruising along, he looked around and said, "What you all looking at me so funny-like for?" which is the way people sometimes are when they've had to climb too high too fast— they can't remember much of anything about what happened while they were up there.

Barry explained it to him, and he didn't even believe it.

"You lost your breakfast," Poetry squawked to him.

"I *did* not," he said, half-angry. He held up an empty ice cream container to prove it, which was a new one the stewardess had brought.

Say! While we were up that high, riding along in the clear blue sunlight, far up above the clouds, it was a strange experience. I looked out the window during the storm and there it was away down below us, with big, black, billowing clouds, which were kinda whitish too, 'cause the sun was shining on them. You could see lightning flashes and even hear thunder roaring. You couldn't see any of the earth at all, nothing but clouds and clouds and clouds, all moving and acting like

they do in any storm, only I was looking *down* at them instead of *up*. It even looked like Sugar Creek does in the spring when it's at high flood and is spread all over the country with high waves boiling and churning and very angry.

At last we were in Chicago, with the plane coming down in the big air field there. It was a sight to see so many planes all around everywhere, with big mail trucks and things and a station almost twice as big as the one we'd started from, ten times as big, in fact.

Pretty soon we were all coming, one at a time, down the little portable stairway, and going through the gate and into the station, where there was a big waiting room and a restaurant.

"I'm hungry," Dragonfly said the very first thing.

People were everywhere all around us, some sitting on the waiting benches, others standing and talking, and many of them in the restaurant eating. "I'm *terribly* hungry," Dragonfly said. And I said, "Which proves that you lost your breakfast up there in the sky."

He glared at me and denied it again, and I knew there wasn't any use to try to convince him.

Then, all of a sudden, we saw Santa Claus coming toward us, a big, round man with a big, round face, and a big smile and a laugh that made everybody else want to laugh too.

Santa Claus, you know, is the name we'd given the jolly man we'd met up north on our camping trip, and who had invited Circus to come to Chicago to sing in his church and over a special radio program which his church has. Of course none of the gang believed there was a real Santa Claus, 'cause our parents didn't believe in telling us there was when there wasn't—and isn't, and never was. Christmas is the time to celebrate the time when The One who had made the world had come down to live here for thirty-three years, and He became a little baby, to begin with.

Pretty soon some of us were in Santa's big car, and the rest of us were in a taxicab which was painted yellow and black, and we were all whirling along very fast through the city. It seemed faster even than being in the plane, 'cause we were meeting other cars which were going just as fast in the other direction and in almost every other direction at the same time, it seemed. Part of the time we were going maybe forty miles an hour, twenty or less the rest of the time, or else were standing still waiting for the car in front of us to move, which was waiting for the car in front of it, which was waiting for the same reason.

For the first time in my life I saw what is called an elevated train, which actually runs along on a track away up above the street. It didn't seem to have any engine to pull it, but was run by electricity, and it twisted its way around above

the streets and cut across corners and in between buildings, some of which were almost as high as four times as high as the tallest trees along Sugar Creek. The elevated, which they called it for short, in fact, they even call it the L for still shorter, and which had sometimes as many as seven or eight or even more long cars, reminded me of my mom using a big needle which she was pushing around, in and out of a pair of Dad's socks which needed darning at the heels, only the L was like a great big giant needle with *joints*, some of which were bent one way and some the other, and all at the same time, threading its way between the different-sized buildings and not bumping into any of them.

Well, Dragonfly wasn't the only one of us who was hungry. The first thing Santa and Barry did was to take us all to a place called *The Southern Tea Shop*, which is in a very old building that was built by a man named Julian Ramsey who used to be mayor of Chicago and was even president of the Corn Exchange Bank there and treasurer of Cook County, but is dead now. He had built the house right after the famous Chicago fire had burned his other one down. That big fire had burned almost all the rest of the city at the same time. Say, that fire had actually been started by a cow kicking over an old-fashioned lantern in a barn. When I heard that, I decided to be more careful not to let our old Brindle

cow do something like that to our lantern at home.

They didn't seem to have any barns in Chicago, though, and certainly not any cows. People there got their milk out of bottles, which grew on their front porch steps every morning. Of course they didn't *actually*, but anybody who could believe in Santa Claus, could believe that too.

Well, there we were in the Tea Shop, all sitting around neat little tables. Over in a corner near a big window, standing on a radiator, I think it was, although I can't remember, was a bright, brass, funny-looking thing which I knew my mom would like to see, 'cause she was always interested in what is called "antiques." We found out it was an old Russian teakettle which had a place for burning charcoal to get the water hot. Of course nobody used it anymore.

After waiting far too long for Dragonfly to wait any longer, our dinner was carried in. Boy, oh boy! Southern fried chicken and hot biscuits, all we could eat! All the time a waitress with the white apron and the white cap on kept going from table to table, bringing more biscuits or water or whatever we wanted. You can believe me that I was glad my parents had made me read a book on etiquette, which tells how to eat with good manners. Even though I didn't always remember to have one hundred percent good manners at our table at home, I would have been

terribly embarrassed not to know how to eat in a fancy place like that. I felt very sorry for little Tom Till, 'cause he didn't know which spoon to take first, the one on the right or the left of the three or four we had, but he was a wise little guy. I watched him out of the corner of my eye and whenever he didn't know how to do something, he looked out of the corner of *his* eye to see how the rest of us were doing it, and then he'd do it the same way. And do you know what? That little guy was watching me more than he was any of the rest of us, and I felt proud to think I could set a good example for him.

I never saw any boy so quick to catch on to things. All the time, though, he was using another corner of his eye to look at people who walked past the window outside. There was a sad expression on his face which meant maybe he was thinking of his brother Bob who might be in Chicago somewhere. Whenever he saw a policeman, or saw a patrol car go past, he looked bothered.

After dinner, we all went to a YMCA. After resting awhile, we went in swimming in water that was clean all the way to the bottom. After that, we sat around in a sort of club room, and made plans for different things to do. There would be time to do only a dozen or more important things, not nearly all we'd planned when we were at home. For Little Jim's sake, we decided

to let him ride on an escalator. Besides that, we'd have time to visit the famous Field Museum, and the Planetarium, and the stockyards and Chinatown, and we could ride to different places on the L.

On Sunday morning early, we were going to visit a jail where there would be boys who hadn't been trained up in the way they ought to go. We'd all give our testimonies there, and Circus would sing. When Santa mentioned "jail," I looked sidewise at Tom, and he swallowed, and his freckled face looked red, but he didn't say a word.

That night we were going to a rescue mission where we'd see a lot of *men* who had grown up, not having been trained in the way *they* should have been.

We decided on Little Jim's escalator first, and got that over with. Say, there were more people in that one big store than lived in all Sugar Creek. Just for fun, most of us boys rode up and down either behind or directly in front of Little Jim. It *is* fun just to walk up to a stairway, right out in the middle of a great big store, and see the stairway slowly going up, all the steps moving at once, and right beside it, coming down, another stairway, each step disappearing the minute it gets to the bottom, and with people coming down on it, not even walking but just getting on a step and standing there.

Barry wouldn't let us do it more than a few times at a time, 'cause escalators were not made to be played on. Well, it was while Little Jim and I were alone once, with him right in front of me, that he showed what kind of thoughts are riding up and down in his pretty curly head most of the time. I was on the step right behind him, and my red head was just as high as his brown one was. In fact, my hand was on his shoulder. "Know what this reminds me of?" he asked, in my ear.

"What?" I said.

"Of the story in the Bible about Jacob's dream." I remember the story 'cause my parents had it in a good Bible storybook which they saw to it that I read regularly instead of a lot of murder stories in what is called comic books. But that doesn't belong to this story. I kept on riding up the escalator with Little Jim, and then at the top we got on the one going down and came down again for the last time. Little Jim knew I was interested in things like that, so he was always waiting for a chance to tell me. In that short minute on the way down, he said, "It reminds me of the story of the ladder Jacob saw in his dream which reached up to heaven and there were angels going up and down on it."

Well, I looked over Little Jim's shoulder to the gang who were waiting for us at the bottom of the escalator—little red-haired, freckle-faced, Tom Till; Circus with his messed-up hair and monkey

face; Poetry, as round as a barrel, and mischievous; Dragonfly with his nose which turns south at the end and his eyes which are too big for his little façe; Big Jim who had shaved his moustache off especially for the Chicago trip, and would probably have to shave again before Christmas.

"What angels?" I asked Little Jim, looking skeptically at the Sugar Creek Gang, which certainly didn't look like angelic beings.

We got to the bottom then, and didn't have a chance to finish what we were talking about, not until we were in the Planetarium.

There were maybe a million things to see in the Planetarium, but it was when we were in the auditorium under the artificial sky with a million stars in it that Little Jim remembered and finished what he wanted to say.

Actually, I never saw such a thing before! The big room where the planetarium machine was is round with seats for hundreds of people. In the center, is the craziest looking man-made thing I ever saw, looking like a skeleton with two heads, one at each end, and with eyes absolutely all over it. It also looks like a great big giant-sized caterpillar, ten feet long and more than a foot thick, with two heads and with eyes on both ends and everywhere. It even looks like a very large ant.

All of a sudden while we were sitting there in the light, the sky, which at first looked like a big

cement dome, began to get dark. At the same time a lady with a very pleasant voice began explaining things to us, all about the astronomy of the thing, with more words, and bigger than I knew the dictionary had. Pretty soon, while it was still twilight, stars began to come out in the dome. The caterpillar was throwing the stars up there, yet you couldn't see any lights on the caterpillar at all, only on the sky. The next thing we knew, it was all dark, with stars all over the sky. It was just like it is at night along Sugar Creek, only there weren't any mosquitoes.

Well, it was a wonderful sight, with the stars all moving around in different directions. There was a moon and sometimes a sun, and different planets which I'd read about somewhere, such as Jupiter and Saturn. Saturn looked like a white baseball with some of my mom's white yarn wrapped around it, making what is called a "ring." It also looked like a wide-brimmed white hat.

Pretty soon, while we were sitting there in the dark, Little Jim's hand reached across the arm of his chair and got hold of mine. He leaned over and said, asking a question, "Jacob's ladder reached clear up into heaven, didn't it?"

I whispered back, "Sure. Why?"

Say! Do you know what that little guy had been thinking? He said, "I think that ladder was supposed to represent Jesus, who is the only way to heaven there is, and we can all go up on Him,

and we can all go to heaven *free* if we have Him. All we have to do is to get on and ride, which is maybe the same as being saved by grace.'' Imagine that little guy thinking that all out by himself!

Just that minute the whole sky began to move around in a strange circle, with some stars going one way and some another and the rest of them going in different directions, and the big black ant out in the middle of the auditorium was slowly moving over on its side and twisting around at the same time. For a jiffy the thoughts in my head started going around just like the stars were, so it wasn't until afterward that I remembered a Bible verse that proved Little Jim was right, which he nearly always is.

The only thing wrong with the pretty lady's very interesting talk was that she didn't mention God as having had anything to do with the creating of the heavens and the earth, like the Bible says. Barry explained that to us later, he having been graduated from a genuinely Christian college, and knew all about astronomy and where it came from.

As I said, I didn't get to decide whether Little Jim was right until afterward, which was that same night when we were away down in the slums of the city where there was a famous rescue mission. Say, I guess there never was such an experience just waiting to happen to a boy. Most of us got the surprise of our lives that night

in that famous Pacific Garden Mission, which is the name of the place. None of us expected to see Big Bob Till at the mission, and the minute he saw us, slide down in his seat and hide his face behind a songbook.

6

RIGHT AFTER WE LEFT the Planetarium and before we had supper, which is called dinner in
Chicago, we took a long, winding walk through
the Field Museum. I'm glad I went there first,
before going to the mission that night.

I'll explain why in just a minute.

I'd rather have gone to a park to see if maybe
we could have seen Little Jim's bear there, if it
was, but the museum was close to the Planetarium, so we went there right away. While Barry
and Santa Claus were taking us through, explaining different things to us, I couldn't help but
think we were kinda like the twelve disciples
following, except there were only seven of us.
Field Museum really has the largest and the most
wonderful collection of what is called specimens
in the whole world—of animal and mineral and
vegetable, Barry said. I took down a few notes
which he gave me afterward and this is what he
said, "The exhibits of the Field Museum are
divided into four categories—anthropology, or
the science of mankind; botany, or the science

of plants; zoology, or the science of animals, and geology, the science of minerals.'' Sometime I'll know more about these things.

Well, we walked along what is called Stanley Hall, which is the main passageway of the whole thing, kinda like the midway in a dead circus. The first thing we saw was two fierce-looking dead elephants standing like they were alive and wanted to fight. I saw Circus looking like he wished he could shin right up the leg of one of them like he does a tree along Sugar Creek and then swing around on one of the elephant's trunks and get up on top. Poetry started in right away with a poem, which goes:

> I went to the animal fair,
>   The birds and the beasts were there,
> The gay baboon by the light of the moon
>   Was combing his auburn hair.

That made me think of my dad with his reddish-brownish-blackish moustache and his long, shaggy eyebrows, and I actually saw him with my mind's eyes, standing in our bathroom before the mirror, combing his eyebrows like he does sometimes, and Mom teases him about it.

Poetry rattled on with the poem, and finally ended up with nobody paying much attention to him:

Then just as the clock struck nine,
   The animals formed a line;
First came the monk on the elephant's trunk,
   And invited him down to dine.

The different animals which we saw were all
stuffed with something which made them look
like they were when they were alive. I think the
name of the business which stuffs and mounts
animals is "taxidermy." Many of the animals
were shown in settings that were just like the
kind they live in when they are alive. Some were
from America, some from Africa, some from
Asia, and there were also a lot of skeletons of
many different kinds of animals in the zoological
department. We even saw a big water hole, which
wasn't actual water, which showed a lot of animals. "Mammals," Barry called them. A mam-
mal is any kind of an animal which has a backbone
and whose mother feeds it in the same way our
old Mixy-cat feeds her little kittens.

Poetry counted twenty-three mammals all arranged around the African water hole. Several of
them were very tall giraffes, and one was a rhinoceros with a little bird on its back.

Pretty soon we were past the animals and were
in the botany department which didn't interest us
so much, except that it showed how much human
beings depend on plants for enough to eat.

Then we went to the anthropology part of the

museum. It was interesting to see all the different people of the world living in the same way they do or used to, or anyway the way they were supposed to have lived, when they were alive.

Little Tom Till stood still, once, looking at some people who were like people in Tibet, and all of a sudden he said, "Are all those different people just stuffed dead people, like the animals back there?"

Imagine that!

"Of course not!" Poetry said, astonished. Even Dragonfly looked across the top of his crooked nose and said, "Of course not! They made them out of plaster of paris, or something, and painted them the different colors!" which was the right answer.

In the geology section, we saw skeletons of what are supposed to be curious animals which were supposed to have lived many millions of years ago. I was glad that when I am at home and running lickety-sizzle through the woods toward Sugar Creek, I don't have to be afraid a great big log will suddenly turn out to be a dinosaur's long tail that will swish around and knock me all to smithereens.

Over in another section, the name of which I can't remember, we stopped in front of an eagle's nest, which was about four feet in diameter, and was made out of sticks and twigs and with some soft material in the middle. Right in the

very middle were several baby eagles which were as big as our old red rooster at home, and had fuzz all over them. Up above the nest was the baby eagles' great big mom with fierce-looking eyes, and with wings that would measure about six feet from tip to tip. Clutched in her fierce, long talons was a snowshoe rabbit, which the mother was going to tear up in a minute and feed to her hungry babies. While we were all looking at the eagle's nest and at the white rabbit in the mother's talons, and listening to Barry explain that baby eagles were very stubborn when they got old enough to fly, and wouldn't get out of the nest and try their wings, and how the mother bird had to stir the nest all up and almost push them off the edge of the cliff, I looked around to see if that had given Little Jim any ideas of his own, and say, that little fellow was looking up at that rabbit dangling there, and there were tears in his eyes. He saw me looking at him, and like he always does when tears get in his eyes, he turned his head, shook it a little; and when I saw his eyes again the tears were gone and were lying somewhere on the marble floor of the museum. As many times in my life as I've seen Little Jim cry a little, I've never seen him use his handkerchief to get rid of his tears.

" 'Smatter?" I asked him on the side.

"N-nothing," he gulped back to me. Then he said, "It's a pretty rabbit, isn't it? It looks like a

lamb." When he said that I knew that maybe in his mind he was spelling the word "lamb" with a capital *L*, and maybe was thinking about the best Friend a boy ever had who had been called the "Lamb of God that taketh away the sin of the world."

After looking at the eagles, we crossed over and saw some birds that are called a Rhinoceros Hornbill. There were two of them, one on the outside of a tree trunk, and the other on the inside, with only its big twelve-inch-long bill sticking out of a small hole. We found out that the one on the outside was the dad and the one on the inside was the mom, and that all daddy hornbills always shut their wives up inside of a hollow tree, and plaster the hole shut except for a very small opening. The mother has to stay inside all the time she is sitting on the nest and until the baby hornbills are hatched and so big they crowd her out.

"You'd think she'd starve to death in there," Poetry said. "Boy! I'm hungry!"

"Starve?" Big Jim said. "Listen to this—" And he read the explanation which was printed on a piece of cardboard on the display cage. And do you know what? That daddy bird with his long yellowish bill, as long as a cow's horn, not only carried mud and stuff and plastered up the hole so his wife couldn't get *out*, and so monkeys and things couldn't get *in* to destroy the nest and

maybe so his wife would be sure to stay at home and look after the children, but he actually worked hard all day long for weeks to find food for her to eat.

Well, I thought, when we all scrambled on to the next exhibit, *Hornbills are very interesting.*

The famous Shedd Aquarium was next. We walked outside the museum, and looked at hundreds of people walking past, or standing on the steps, and looked toward Lake Michigan which wasn't far away. Then we went down to the very wide sidewalk, and through a tunnel under the street and out on the other side, where we all bought and ate some ice cream. At the entrance to the mammoth-sized aquarium, I looked up at the big electric light and it had on it a big starfish carved in stone or iron or something for decoration. Inside, there were people and people and people, and fish and fish and fish of every kind and shape and color of the rainbow. *Live* fish, all of them! Big, little, long, short, flat, pug-nosed, stumpy-tailed, round, with horns, without them, swimming, each kind in its own private aquarium. It was a sight to see, and made me wish I could just once catch one of them on my fishing pole in Sugar Creek.

From the Aquarium we walked on a high cement fence along the lakefront, and shouldn't have, maybe. A great big long wide high cement something-or-other ran out like a bent elbow into

70

the lake very far, and is called a "breakwater" which was supposed to protect the shore and the beach from the terrible force of the waves, especially if there should ever be a windstorm. There were maybe a thousand sea gulls on and off it. Well, we all wanted to take a boat ride in a speedboat, and we did. Boy, oh boy! it was a thrill! Our old boat shot out across the water, and around on the other side of the breakwater where the waves were high and where the spray dashed over the gunwale and made a lot of beautiful little rainbows, which were so close to us that I reached out and stuck my arm into the one that was flying right along with us. Then, just for fun, Poetry took both his big fat hands and clasped them together and said, "Here, Bill, have a chunk of rainbow." I reached out and took it and ate it.

Well, we squealed, and hollered and laughed and got a little bit frightened, especially Little Jim. He had his eyes focused on the edge of the rainbow and I knew he maybe had one in his mind too. He was grinning and holding onto Big Jim, and I heard him say to him, "It's nice to have a rainbow flying right along beside you," and if I'd been a preacher or a minister, I'll bet I could have thought up something interesting for my congregation next Sunday morning.

After the ride, we walked along the waterfront and felt the cool breeze fanning our cheeks, then we came to the boulevard and would have walked

over to the Conrad Hilton Hotel which as I told you is the largest hotel in the world, but the traffic was so fast and so heavy that Barry and Santa made us walk clear back to the aquarium to the tunnel that goes under the street.

It was a long walk, past the museum again and over a high wooden bridge, with a lot of railroad tracks under it and the trains flying along under there every few jiffies; and ahead of us were the great big high buildings of the city, looking like big tall, irregular, lower teeth in some fierce wild animal's mouth. Pretty soon we were at the hotel, and were inside, where we were supposed to write cards or letters to our folks to tell them we had arrived in Chicago without being scared to death. I wrote a *long* letter to my folks, and told them all I could think of about the city. Poetry, who as I told you is an expert in arithmetic, and who is also mischievous, helped me write the letter, and this is what I wrote:

Dear Mom and Dad and pug-nosed Charlotte Ann:

I am now sitting at a desk in the world's largest hotel, a picture of which you will see on the postcard enclosed. Actually, I didn't know such a hotel existed. There are 2,600 guest rooms in it, and if the seven members of the Sugar Creek Gang would decide to sleep in all of them, one night at a time, each one of us having his

own room, it would take all of us over a year and a month to do it. If I wanted to sleep in every one of them myself, it would take me over eight years, and by that time I would have slept on sixty freight carloads of innerspring mattresses. Say, the dining rooms are so big that when they first bought enough plates for them, they had to buy 134,000, besides fifty carloads of other chinaware, enough to fill all the silos on maybe twenty-five farms around Sugar Creek. I could use three napkins a day and it would take me over 273 years to use all of them. They have 138,000 tablecloths, and if all their 48,000 drinking glasses were filled with water at the same time and poured out in Sugar Creek, all at once, it might cause a flood. They have enough silverware to fill all our haymow twice. If you and Mom want to come here sometime, you can not only check your suitcases and come back for them, but you can check Charlotte Ann, and they'll keep her till you come back.

Not only that, but the longest street in this town, which is Western Avenue, is as long as from Sugar Creek to Sandville, which, as you know, is twenty-four miles. They have over 4,851 firemen in the fire department, and they surely need them 'cause it seems like every few minutes I hear a fire engine going past. There are over 3,520,000 people living here and there are more than 1,800 churches. Only about six hundred of them are Protestant churches. Many of them are either Roman or Greek Catholic churches,

and the rest are different kinds of religions. But just think of that! Wait a minute while I get Poetry to stop pinching me under the table.

Say, Dad, do you know what Poetry just said? He said, "I'll betcha that that's why Chicago has so much crime. 'Cause most of the people here stay at home from church as much as Bob Till does."

Poetry is just sitting here reading about the Chicago River in a book, right beside me at the table in this very beautiful room, and he says it is one of the few rivers in the world which flows backward. That is, intead of flowing toward its *mouth* like any decent river should, it goes the other way.

Well, this letter will have to close 'cause tonight we are all going down on South State Street to a famous rescue mission, where many years ago a famous baseball player named Billy Sunday was coverted, and he is the famous evangelist who is dead now. In fact, some people who are now very important in the Christian world were born again at that mission. One of them, Barry told us, was named Mel Trotter, and he went to Grand Rapids, Michigan, and founded what is now the largest city rescue mission in the world.

In fact I have to stop writing right now, 'cause we have to make a visit to the Moody Bible Institute which is the largest Bible institute in the world, and where Circus has to practice singing before a microphone, with Little Jim playing for

him, so he won't be so frightened when he actually sings over the radio. I am having a wonderful time, which I'll tell you about when I get home, especially about the airplane trip. Boy, oh boy—here we go now to Moody Bible Institute.

Wonderfully yours,
BILL COLLINS

7

THAT NIGHT we saw Bob Till. That was while we were at the rescue mission, though, and we didn't get there until after supper which we ate at the Moody Bible Institute, which is the largest Bible institute in the world, as I think I told you before. Thousands and thousands of young people have been trained there to be missionaries, pastors, teachers, choir directors, evangelists and Christian education directors.

Say! We went downstairs with Barry and Santa Claus, whose real name I ought to tell you is the Reverend Don Farmer, and pretty soon we were standing up in front of our plates at a big long table in their dining room. All around us were hundreds and hundreds of people, nearly all young people, and everybody was talking and laughing and smiling, until some soft chimes sounded. Then somebody started a song, which was a church hymn tune, using the words:

> Be present at our table, Lord,
> Be here and everywhere adored;

> These mercies bless, and grant that we
> May feast in paradise with Thee.

It was the first time I'd ever thought about there going to be something good to eat when we got to heaven, and I thought it was a good idea, 'cause I was terribly hungry right that minute. So also was Poetry who was always hungry anyway, and so also was Dragonfly who had only digested one meal that day. In a few seconds there was a quiet scraping of about one thousand chairs as one thousand people in that great big dining room sat down, and waited to be served. Again I was glad I knew my manners, and not only knew them but had had sense enough to practice them at home so I didn't look awkward in a public place like that.

Pretty soon supper was over, and the one thousand people started getting up from the different tables and going out. Upstairs in what is called the lobby of the women's building, we met a lot of different people, such as the president of the school, and the dean of men, and the director of the radio where Circus was going to sing, and where in a few minutes, he was going to practice.

Rooms, rooms, rooms, people, people, people, and nearly everybody was carrying a Bible under his arm, or in his hand, just like children do in school when they carry their schoolbooks. I reached into my vest pocket and took out my

own little thin New Testament and carried it, out where people could see that I wasn't ashamed of it.

Then we went to the administration building, and into an elevator, and all of us crowded in, Barry and Mr. Farmer and all of us taking off our different kinds of hats or caps, whichever we'd worn, cause there was a lady on the elevator too. Up, up we went, stopping at every floor to see if there was anybody else who wanted to get on, and pretty soon we were away up in the radio tower, and in a little room. In a few jiffies, Circus and Little Jim were ready to practice. The piano was what is called a baby grand, and it surely looked nice. The microphone which stood on a long brasslike stem, was round and looked kinda like a small steering wheel on an automobile. Circus had learned his song by heart, and so had Little Jim which is the way to make a song sound better when you're singing it and so, if people are watching you sing, you can look them right in the eyes and make them listen better.

None of us knew, of course, that Mr. Farmer had a surprise planned for us that night in his apartment. But that comes later.

Moody Bible Institute, we found out, is not only the largest Bible institute in the world, but the radio which has its studios in the tower of their twelve-story building, is dedicated, as Old Man Paddler will be very glad to know, "wholly

to the service of the Lord Jesus Christ.'' Before we left there that night, to go to the mission, they handed us some literature telling about the school, which I sent home to my mom and dad, and Poetry sent home the same to his parents.

I could just see my mom and dad sitting at our kitchen table, with Charlotte Ann in her bassinet beside them, and nobody sitting at my place. I'll bet they'd have my chair there, though, and maybe my plate and my favorite blue mug out of which I drank milk three times a day. And Dad would open my letter from Chicago and read it and then he'd say, ''Wow! Look at this about the Moody Bible Institute! It says there are 65,000 people who study the Bible by mail from there!''

Then my mom might lean over and they'd read it together, with his bushy red hair and her kinda brownish-gray hair brushing against each other. And this is what they'd read:

Faculty of 81 teachers.

Library of over 66,000 volumes.

More than 1,000 students in the day school and 980 in the evening school each year.

A magazine with 112,620 paid subscribers.

Radio, the school's own 5,000-watt station broadcasting over 200 programs a week.

More than 4,640 former students have gone to be missionaries in 107 foreign fields.

Well, my parents would also be glad to know that Little Jim had already made up his mind he wanted to go to school there some time.

As soon as Little Jim and Circus had finished practicing, we all went over to what is called the "153 Building" and up to a room which is called "Mr. Moody's Room," where they have different things about Dwight L. Moody's life, the man who started the school in the first place. There were a lot of things to see, such as a chair they wouldn't let anybody sit in, 'cause it was Moody's old chair.

To me the most interesting thing was a picture of a gang of fourteen ragged-looking boys who belonged to Moody's first Sunday school many years ago. They were sitting or half-sitting down, or standing, and one of them had a worn-out broom standing in front of him.

"What crazy names," Poetry said, reading some of them out loud, each boy's crazy name being printed right below him. I listened to Poetry's squawky voice calling off the ridiculous names, and this is what some of them were:

"Red Eye, Smikes, Butcher, Rag Breeches—" Rag Breeches is the one who had the broom. There were fourteen all together. Right above the gang of boys, was printed "BEFORE," which means the way the boys looked when Moody got them to start to Sunday school.

Then, right beside that picture was the same

gang of boys, and they had their hair combed and had on new suits, which some rich Christian in Chicago had paid for. The boys earned the suits by going to Sunday school quite a while. There was certainly a difference in the looks of the two pictures.

All of a sudden, Little Tom Till, who was standing at my right elbow, piped up and said, "What happened to the *other* two?"

"What other two?" I said, and then I looked, and sure enough he was right. On the first picture, the one called "BEFORE," there were fourteen boys, and on the other picture, entitled "AFTER," there were only twelve.

"Maybe they stopped going to Sunday school," Little Jim said.

In a jiffy my mind was astray, wondering what became of those two extra boys, and what kind of parents they had. I hoped none of our gang would ever stop going to Sunday school, and drop out of the picture.

Pretty soon after that we were on a bus going to the mission. Circus and I sat together on one of the seats. The rest of us were on one side or the other, with a lot of different-looking people all around and in front of us and behind us, some being Negroes and some Italians, some Greeks, one a Jew and another, right across from us, a Japanese; and I thought that if anybody wanted to be a missionary and for some reason didn't get to

go to a foreign country, he could be one right in Chicago.

Say, all of a sudden Little Jim got up out of his seat, and kinda balanced himself a little, holding on to the seat tops, then he staggered forward two or three seats and handed a piece of paper to a little Negro boy who was sitting there beside his mom. Little Jim acted very bashful while he slipped back to his seat beside Mr. Farmer, he being the only one of us who could actually sit beside him without having to put a foot out into the edge of the aisle to keep from falling off. Well, now maybe that statement was what is called exaggeration, but Santa, or Mr. Farmer, is a very big man, anyway.

At last there we were, just about two blocks from the mission, which two blocks we would have to walk. I guess I never saw so many people in my life who looked like they were prodigal sons, and who ought to go back home and get cleaned up, as well as to confess their sins and get their souls washed.

We walked along like people do in cities, everybody walking very fast and in a terrible hurry to get somewhere from somewhere. Not at all like people do in Sugar Creek who know they are alive and that the world isn't going to fall to pieces tomorrow.

Down those two blocks, all along the side of the sidewalk, were the filthiest-looking theaters

and old saloons and dirty men who couldn't walk straight, and whose breath you could smell without getting close to them. And everywhere were electric signs doing all kinds of things, whirling in circles, jabbing back and forth like arrows, zigzagging like a football player dodging through a crowd of other players, blinking on and off, and on and off and keeping on doing it without ever stopping. Most of the signs advertised beer or liquor of some kind, or cheap rooms.

Pretty soon we were there, getting a drink out of a bubbling little water fountain just outside the door.

In the display window of the mission, which was like a big long store building, was a sign, *How Long Since You Wrote to Mother?* There was also a big Bible, wide open, with a verse marked for people to read. Poetry was already reading the verse out loud in his squawky voice, which was half boy's voice and half man's. It was the verse which begins, "I will arise and go to my father, and will say unto him, 'Father, I have sinned. . . .' "

Just inside the door, a smiling man handed us a hymnbook which was the same kind we used in our church at home. Then the superintendent who was a tall, smiling, big-voiced man not more than thirty years old, led us all the way up the long aisle to the front, up the platform stairs, which had been freshly polished, and across the

platform, on each side of which was a great big grand piano, and into an office in the back, where there was a man at a desk. We left our different kinds of caps in the office.

Santa had us all sit down, 'cause he was going to preach at the mission there that night, and some of the men of his church were going to give their testimonies, his church being the kind of a church that was alive enough to have what is called a gospel team, like the one our church has at Sugar Creek and which my dad is the leader of.

There was a prayer meeting in the office before we began the mission meeting itself; and all of us got down on our knees with the superintendent and Barry and Santa.

Then, up we got and out we went and pretty soon were sitting on the platform between the two big pianos. I wished Little Jim could have played one of the pianos, but they already had a man sitting on each piano bench, and I knew Little Jim would have to wait until Circus' solo before he would get to play.

It would take too long to tell every interesting thing that happened, so I'll skip some of it. Of course I felt proud of Little Jim while he played the piano for Circus' solo. Circus' voice sounded even sweeter than when he is singing from a treetop along Sugar Creek. His pretty brown hair actually glistened under the big electric light above

his head, and the people out in the long audience acted like they couldn't move, and didn't want to anyway. I always liked to sit on a platform and look out at all the different people's different kinds of faces, like I do at a big herd of cattle in a field, which stand still and look at you if you happen to have on a red sweater. Circus' voice really was wonderful.

I never will forget what the big, tall, smiling superintendent said, when Circus finished. He stood there very tall and straight for a minute after Circus had sat down, and then he said to the people, "It's unusual to see a fine boy like this using his voice for the Lord, instead of singing the music of the world." He turned to Circus and made him stand up beside him. Then he put his arm halfway around him like my tall dad does me when he likes me or is proud of me for something, and he said to the people, "How many of you will pledge yourselves to pray for this young man, that God will make him a mighty power in the world for winning souls?" I looked at Circus through the superintendent's eyes and he actually looked like a young man. Then I looked at myself through my own eyes and I didn't look like very much, only a red-headed kid with too many freckles, and I wasn't growing fast enough.

Well, in answer to the superintendent's question, I saw nearly every hand in the crowd go up to pray for Circus—the hands of the nice-looking

Christian people who were there to visit the mission, and some of the dirty, wrinkled-up old hands of some of the drunkards and of the other men. Some of the drunkards had been half asleep and some had just been shut up for talking out loud in church.

Well, at Pacific Garden Mission they never have what is called a "formal service," but they act like a great big family, and sometimes they are even noisy, but it seemed like all the Christian people there loved God with all their hearts. Over on the right side of the mission and about halfway back to the door with the glass panel in it, sat about three rows of young people who had come there from some church in Chicago to visit and to give their testimonies when it was time for them to do it.

Say, all of a sudden, right in the middle of the testimony meeting, a man stood up right under the great big picture of Billy Sunday which was hanging on the wall over the heads of the young people, and with a loud gruff and very husky voice started in to tell everybody what a terrible drunkard he had been once and had tried to quit drinking for many years and couldn't. "And then, one night," he said, "when I was about to kill myself, and was staggering around on the street, I heard music which was coming right through that door there and—"

Talk about being glad he was saved! That man

certainly sounded like it. In fact, he waved his arms and walked out into the aisle and talked so fast and so hard that for a minute he reminded me of a man in a prizefight. In fact, he had been a prizefighter once. He had a crooked nose that was also flat.

The next man who testified looked like a very important businessman, with pretty white hair and a good shave. He talked quietly and very kindly.

It was when they were taking the collection, or rather when *we* were that we saw Bob Till come in at the door and sit down on a back seat. I say when "we" were taking the collection, 'cause the superintendent asked two of the Sugar Creek Gang to do it. He looked around at us who were sitting behind him and picked out Big Jim and me, and handed us the offering plates which looked like two of my mom's new bright tin baking pans.

I'd never helped take an offering before, so I felt a little embarrassed at first, but proud, too. We started at the front and were working our way back to the rear, most people not giving anything 'cause many of them didn't have anything to give, some of them having come in on purpose so they could have a place to sleep that night. They were supposed to be there at fifteen minutes past eight or before they couldn't have a bed to sleep on. Talk about a bed! But I'll tell you about that in a jiffy.

I didn't have more than seventy-five cents in my offering plate, or pan, I should say, when I was almost back to the back of the room, when all of a sudden I looked, and there was a ten-dollar bill in it, which a drunken man had dropped in, most drunken men nearly always being glad to give their money away or else drink it up, or buy drinks for anybody else that wants them.

Right that minute the door opened, and Bob Till staggered in. I couldn't believe my eyes, and yet there he was, slithering into a seat in a corner right in front of me. I was still taking the collection, and was facing the door, so I could see Bob. He kinda melted down into his seat and ducked his head.

8

I LEANED OVER and whispered, "Hi, Bob!"

Say! His head shot up like he was startled, and I felt funny inside. You could have knocked me over with an exclamation point, I was so surprised. The two pianos on the platform were playing a duet, with somebody accompanying them on a violin, so nobody but us could hear what we said to each other.

Say! I guess you could have knocked *him* over with a comma or maybe a period. He turned white and stared at me, and then at the money in the offering plate, looking like he had seen a red-haired, freckle-faced ghost. He didn't actually look very much like Bob, though, for his face was dirty, and his hair was combed on a different side and at the same time looked messed up like mine does when I've been standing on my head in our front yard at home.

"SHHH!" Bob said. "Don't tell anybody who I am. The police—" He slid down into his seat, grabbed a songbook and buried his face in it, and for some reason I began to feel very sorry for

him. Anyway, I was sorry for his brother Tom, so I kept still. Big Jim hadn't even noticed him, so we walked back up to the platform with our offering plates, and sat down again and watched the meeting. The more I looked back to the back row to where Bob Till was, the more I realized that he didn't look like himself at all, and maybe I was the only one of the gang who would recognize him, I thought.

Just that minute I felt Poetry nudge me in the side and he said, "Look who's on the back row!"

"Shhh!" I said, and glanced out of my eye at Little Tom Till. I really didn't know what to do. I wondered why Bob was staying inside when he knew we were there.

Poetry whispered to me again and said, "I'll bet he doesn't know *we* know about the stolen money from Mr. Simondson's grocery or he'd beat it out into the street and hide somewhere."

I hadn't thought of that. Of course he didn't know, I thought, so I kept on keeping still, and the meeting went on to its close.

Well, I'd seen people take their suitcases into railroad depots or into hotels and check them, and get a little round check with a number on it, and then come back later and hand the check to the baggage man, and get back the suitcases, but I'd never heard of a man taking *himself* to a mission and checking *himself*, but that's exactly what happened. Pretty soon there began a slow,

sad parade of sad-faced men walking past us, to the platform, each one taking a little round check with a number on it, and walking across the platform to the stair door.

Such men I'd never even seen, or read about. I mean such unhappy men. It really was a terrible sight to see—all kinds of men with all kinds of shaped heads, and different-lengthed, different-colored hair, all of their hair needing to be washed, and also their faces. They all had different kinds of eyes, some of which were all bleary, and there wasn't a one which had a twinkle in it. Some of the men looked very fierce, some very sad, and some were slouched over and acted like they wished they weren't alive, which Dad says is the way anybody feels who doesn't have any hope. Only a few of them looked like they were actually alive in their souls.

Thinking about that made me wonder why anybody ever wanted to hire out to the devil in the first place, if that was the kind of wages he paid all his hired men.

Well, pretty soon I saw Bob Till coming, and he had his hair pulled down over his eyes, and his short collar turned up about his neck. His head was down and he looked for a jiffy at Big Jim and at the same time I looked down and saw Bob's fists double up and I knew he hated Big Jim. I looked quick at the rest of our gang and

Poetry was the only one who had recognized Bob. Even Tom didn't know him.

In another jiffy Bob had his check and was up on the platform following the others. I watched him until he was gone. Then I looked around and none of the gang looked like they'd seen anybody they knew. About six minutes later, we were allowed to go upstairs to watch the men go to bed.

Barry and Mr. Farmer went up with us, also one of the workers of the mission. It was not only interesting to see, but it was absolutely the unhappiest thing I ever saw. Not a man was smiling and nobody acted like he was glad he was alive.

The man who had given them their checks was up there too, going from one cot to another getting their names, and putting each name down beside the number of his check. Men, men, men, all over.

"I don't think that's Bob," Poetry said to me, and I looked again, and decided maybe Poetry was right.

Just before we left, the man who'd been taking names, stopped at one of the cots and said to the man lying there, "Hey, buddy, put your head down at *this* end!"

I didn't like that, 'cause I thought a man had a right to put his head at whichever end of the bed he wanted to, but Barry explained it. "The law

says that they have to sleep so they can't breathe or cough in any other man's face. That's a health law," and then I understood.

Boy, oh boy, I thought about my nice, soft mattress at home in our upstairs, and the cool, clean sheets, and of my swell mom who always had my bed turned down for me at night, and for a minute I couldn't see straight, for some crazy old tears kept getting mixed up in my eyes. Just that minute I looked at Little Jim and I saw him turn his face away and give his grand little curly head a toss, and I knew that somewhere on that wooden floor would be a couple of tears.

Pretty soon we were all going down the stairs to the main floor, and to the street, and finally to Santa's apartment, where at midnight we had a very strange surprise waiting for us.

At the door though, we stopped and they let us look over the list of names of the men who were upstairs, and would you believe it? There were five men who had the same name, and that name was "Frank Smith."

"Who *are* they?" Dragonfly asked. "Are they all brothers, or what?"

"Nobody knows who they are," the mission man said. "We get a lot of men by that name." There was even a man named John Doe on the list. I let my eye slide down the whole page and there wasn't anybody there named Bob Till, ei-

ther, so I knew if it really was him, he had given a false name.

Outside the mission we all stopped to get a drink at the little drinking fountain, the Chicago water not tasting as good to us as the water from the spring at Sugar Creek. Say, when I looked up from getting my drink, there was a police car parking right in front of the mission. Two big burly policemen climbed out and walked up to the door. They gave us boys all a very careful looking over before they let us go, then they went into the mission, and we went on to Santa's apartment, each one of us thinking his own thoughts.

On the way home we stopped in a part of the city called Chinatown, where many Chinese people live, and where I bought a pound of tea. I asked the Chinese clerk to wrap it up and send it to my mom, who liked Chinese tea very much.

In another store, we saw a half-dozen men sitting around a table, each one had a little pile of American money in front of him and they were playing some kind of game with little yellow cubes with Chinese characters on them, the cubes looking like little pieces of cream cheese. In another store, a man was mixing perfume, and in another, we saw a great big Chinese dragon, as long as our barn at home, and all colored, and it looked like a big rainbow which had been straightened out, only it had a fierce head with savage

eyes. We couldn't stay very long in Chinatown, but it surely was interesting, and once I saw a very cute little black-haired Chinese boy in the street, very mischievous, and with some tourists standing around in a little half-circle, watching him and laughing at things he said and did. His Chinese mom, who was very pretty, was watching him too, and acting very proud of him, just like my mom does when people look at Charlotte Ann and tell her how cute she is.

In the car, on the way to Santa's apartment, Santa said, "You ought to see a Chinese Sunday school sometime. We have over fifty teachers, one teacher for every student."

They talked about that awhile, but Poetry and I still had our thoughts on Bob Till, and wondered to each other what the police wanted to go into the mission for. We found out Sunday morning when we went to visit a boys' jail.

9

AT SANTA'S APARTMENT, we had our strange surprise, and Little Jim taught me another important lesson. Mrs. Santa, or rather, Mrs. Farmer—I was learning to call her that—met us with a smile and a gurgling giggle that was very cheerful. She introduced us to their canary bird, Cheery, which was trained and could be let out of the cage and would fly around from room to room. It would stand on a dresser in front of a mirror and act very angry at its reflection, not knowing maybe, that it was seeing only its very pretty yellow self.

All over the apartment were a lot of cots for us to sleep on. Santa's study had two cots in it, as well as a library. Mrs. Farmer was as tickled to see all of us as if we had been her own boys, which, just for fun, she said we were. She had sandwiches ready for us, and gave each of us a glass of milk and after a half hour or more, we all went to bed.

It was funny to see us all decked out in our different colored pajamas, all ready to climb into our cots. Poetry's pajamas were white with reddish-

purple stripes running around them, which made him look like a fat prisoner from some jail. We would have teased the life out of him if we hadn't all remembered Bob Till, and felt sorry for little red-haired Tom, so that joke was spoiled. Pretty soon we had sung a chorus and had said our prayers, each one saying his own quietly beside his own bed, then we climbed in and the lights went out.

I was certainly tired. Dragonfly was in a cot right beside me in the study, but I went right off to sleep and into a crazy dream, with plenty of things scrambling around in my mind—canary birds and stars and dinosaurs and dragons and fish. Then I turned into a giant-sized needle and was darning Dad's socks, when I was awakened by somebody at the window in our room, standing out there on a fire escape, and dressed in a striped prison suit. Well, it didn't make sense, and was part of my silly dream, I thought, so I didn't believe it. Not until who-ever it was began to rattle the window and to crawl inside, the screen having been taken off already.

Dragonfly woke up scared, and pretty soon everybody in all the rooms were awake. The lights were turned on, and it was Poetry himself.

"Just a new way to wake people up," he said. He stood there in our room, and yawned and acted indifferent, until Dragonfly decided to throw

a pillow at him. That made us all decide to do the same thing, which we did.

But it was all a part of the surprise Santa had planned for us. We were supposed to be awakened at midnight to listen to a special midnight broadcast from the radio station we'd visited.

Pretty soon we were out in the biggest room where the canary had been but wasn't now, he having been put in a covered cage in the kitchen.

Santa turned on the radio while we found places to sit in chairs and on each other's cots, and pretty soon the program was on. We'd been listening for only about a few minutes when I heard somebody playing the piano, very beautifully, and then all of a sudden somebody began to sing, and it was a voice *exactly* like Circus' voice, as clear as a bell, high and very resonant. I looked around quick, and there was Circus with a very funny expression on his already funny face. Then he scowled and acted bashful. Sure enough it was his voice.

Yet it couldn't have been! 'Cause there he was, right in front of my eyes, looking sleepy and wide awake and bashful at the same time. And there was Little Jim, too.

"It's *canned* music," Santa said. "They made a transcription when you were in the studio right after dinner."

It surely was a beautiful song:

> My sins are forgiven, I know
> My sins are forgiven, I know,
> Not through works of my own,
> But through Jesus alone,
> My sins are forgiven, I know.

They'd made that transcription, and Circus and Little Jim hadn't known it, which if they had they'd probably have made a fizzle instead. All the way through the four stanzas of the solo I kept thinking how very much I'd give if I could have been Circus or Little Jim, and have had what is called a "transcription" made of something important which I could do.

But I really couldn't do anything important—not like singing or playing a piano or some other musical instrument. I was just old freckle-faced, red-haired William Jasper Collins who hadn't even learned how to control his temper, and I didn't even have good manners except when I wasn't at home. There was Little Jim and Circus, who'd already decided what they were going to be when they were grown up. One was going to be a gospel singer, and the other a missionary, and I—then I remembered that I was going to be a doctor, and a genuinely *Christian* doctor at that, and perform operations on people. But you couldn't have an electrical transcription made of an appendicitis operation. So I felt sad.

All the time I was thinking that, and maybe

shouldn't have been, 'cause it was selfish to, the song kept going on, "My sins are forgiven, I know, My sins are forgiven, I know, My sins are forgiven, I know."

Just then Little Jim slid over to me from the other end of the cot he and I were sitting on, and I looked down at his pretty little mouse-shaped face to see if he was proud of himself, and he wasn't. I know, 'cause he leaned over and whispered in my ear one of the prettiest things I'd ever heard or ever thought of in my whole life. And this is it: "Do you know what I'm thinking about?" he squeaked.

Or course I didn't, so I asked him, "What?"

He waited till there was what is called an interlude between stanzas, which was piano music only, and then he said, "All those eighty-eight piano keys, from one end to the other, are going to be Little *Jim's* ladder, reaching up to heaven, and each one will be a gospel step for people to go up on."

It was after that that I was ashamed of myself for wanting to be famous, so I tried to think of what I could do with a surgeon's knife that would help people's *souls*. There are a lot of people in the world, and right even in Sugar Creek, who ought to have their *hearts* operated on.

Well, after the surprise, we all had to have a dish of homemade ice cream, which was already made and in the refrigerator waiting for us. Then

we went to bed again and to sleep, and the next thing I knew it was morning, with another whole day ahead of us, and still another one after that, and with our most exciting adventure still unhappened, the one that was a little bit like the dream I'd had at Sugar Creek that day when I was pouring raspberry juice into a boy's blood veins through a little tin funnel. Never in my life will I forget what happened, and why—and neither will Big Jim and Big Bob Till, 'cause it happened to both of them.

10

THE NEXT DAY was Saturday. We did a lot of things and saw even more than we did. The very first thing we did was to go to the Brookfield Zoo, where we looked especially to see if we could see Little Jim's pet bear, which had had a white triangle on its chest, but we didn't find it. Say, you ought to see that zoo! Honest, there are more live things to look at and laugh at than you can see anywhere else in Chicago, especially the monkeys.

Once when we were standing in front of a bear's cage watching three fuzzy baby bears eating their dinner in the way mammals do, for a minute I imagined I was back home listening to a million honeybees droning in the old linden tree which grows near the spring. If you've ever heard baby bears eat their dinner like that, you know they sound like that. I could, for a minute, almost smell the perfume of the pretty creamy-yellow linden flowers I was thinking about. That is, until I smelled the bears' den.

The fuzzy little bears reminded Poetry of a

poem which is good enough for me to write down for you. Here it is, quoted in his more-than-ever-squawky voice:

> Fuzzy-wuzzie wuz a bear,
> Fuzzy-wuzzie had no hair;
> Fuzzy-wuzzie wuzn't fuzzy,
>> Wuz he?

If you say that real fast, it sounds funny, and is.

Halsted Street! I never saw anything like it. We were looking out the windows and seeing everything we could see. Even the grocery stores in Chicago sell whiskey, I noticed. There were hundreds of trucks and trailers going both directions, and all along the way were hundreds of sad-looking, dirty-faced store buildings, with people living in their upstairs, the saddest and dirtiest ones being the ones that were closed and for rent. The windows of the car were open, so with all the traffic, it was just roar, roar, roar all the time like the Sugar Creek threshing machine in the harvest, when you're up close to it.

Well, we saw different things while we were walking. On the lawn of a big building called the Exchange Building was a sculptured stone bust of Abraham Lincoln, the sixteenth President of the United States.

Just as we walked past, Barry, who was be-

hind us, said, "Boys, Abraham Lincoln was a farm boy. When he was your age he hunted, fished, rode horseback, wrestled, and studied hard. He could shoot very straight with a rifle, and he made that a rule of his life—to be what is called a 'straight shooter,' which means he was always honest. In fact, he was called 'Honest Abe' by his friends."

I really can't take time to tell you all the things we saw, but it was worth the walk all right—and also worth the smell, although inside the entrance office of the particular packing plant we were going to see, the air was very fresh and clean, on account of the office being what is called air-conditioned, which means the air is actually washed before it is pumped into the office buildings.

Ho-hum! It was interesting enough, but some of it was what Big Jim said was *gruesome*. If you don't know what that means, you can look it up in a good dictionary, which every boy ought to have anyway, and ought to save his money and buy one, even if he has to do without some candy and gum to buy it.

11

Well, that was that. We ate dinner in a
Swedish restaurant where you can eat all you want,
if you want to. You can get up after you've had
your first plateful and go back with a new, clean
plate which they give you, and eat all over again,
which some of us did. I think the name of that
kind of a dinner is called "smorgasboard." Poetry especially thought it was a good idea.

The Wrigley Building was next, and while we
were up in it there, we looked down at a very
large parking lot which looked very small, and
the many colored automobiles away down there
looked like toy automobiles.

"Look!" Dragonfly said, squeezing in between
Poetry and me. "They look like a counter full of
toy cars in a dime store," which they did, and
for once Dragonfly's eyes were right.

Well, that afternoon flew past too fast, and
also that night, and then Sunday morning came,
when we all went to a boys' jail, and there we
found out why the police had gone into the mission that night. They were actually after Bob Till

and they actually found him upstairs on the third floor lying on one of the cots.

I guess I never saw Little Tom Till look so sad in my life, 'cause sitting right on the front row of a big roomful of hundreds of boys who hadn't been trained up in the way they ought to go, sat Bob, looking down and looking very unhappy. His nose, I noticed for the first time, was hooked a little at the end just like his dad's nose is, and I thought that maybe his soul was just as crooked, only it was his dad who had bent it for him.

But say! Little Tom had good stuff in him! He stood up right after Circus had sung his solo, and told all that big crowd of quiet-faced boys how he became a Christian and when, and why he was glad of it. You remember it had happened while we were all on our camping trip up north that summer. He didn't even shed a tear, but he must have felt very topsy-turvy inside 'cause he kept swallowing to keep his throat damp. His brother Bob, sitting down there in front of us on the front row, had his fists all doubled up with one on his right knee and the other on his left. Then he began to swallow too, and to blow his nose with his handkerchief, which is what a boy does when there are tears trying to get out of his eyes and some of them run down on the *inside* of his nose instead of on the *outside*. That's why nearly all people have to blow their noses when they cry for some reason.

It was when Big Jim was standing up there giving the story of his conversion, which means when and how and why he became a Christian, that I realized how different he and Bob were. They were the same size and age but that was about all. And not only that. Say, it was Poetry who was sitting beside me that called something to my attention. He leaned over and whispered while Big Jim was talking, "Look! Look at Bob's fists. They are all doubled up!"

They *certainly* were, and there were two fires in his eyes too. You could see that Bob hated Big Jim, and that he wished he could spring right up out of his seat and knock the daylights out of him. You see, Big Jim was the only boy in the world who had ever licked Bob. The *only* one. Of course, Big Jim's being a swell guy, and with clean habits didn't help things either.

Things began to happen fast after that. After the meeting was over, Barry and Mr. Farmer and the authorities at the jail talked awhile and there was some telephoning going on between Chicago and Sugar Creek, and the next thing we knew Bob Till was free. It happened that quick, although I found out afterward that there had been some telephoning going on during the night before also. Old Man Paddler had wanted Bob to be let out on parole 'cause it wasn't good for a boy to be sent to jail for his first offense. They were going to parole him to Little Jim's parents, and

he was going to work for them that fall. Mr. Simondson, our grocer, had decided not to do what is called "bring charges," so Bob got out of jail.

The result was that when we all left there that morning, Big Bob was walking along with us. He even had on a new suit which Barry had bought. The only thing was, he kept giving Big Jim dirty looks all the time. I kept walking right along beside them while we went to our car, 'cause I didn't trust Bob. The reason was, that once when I was close to them, I heard Bob swear at Big Jim under his breath and say, "Think you're smart, don't you? Telling people you saw me break into that store."

"I *did* not!" Big Jim said, and his upper lip was trembling.

"You did *too!* As soon as I get a chance, you'll find out Bob Till won't stand for anybody telling lies on him!"

Just then we came to our car, and Big Jim and Bob had to separate. I sat beside Big Jim on the way to church, and so I said, looking at his moustacheless upper lip while I said it, "You certainly didn't tell any lies on Bob, did you?"

"Of course not," he said. "Nor any truths either. I didn't tell anybody *any*thing, but he thinks I did 'cause I saw him with my own eyes running out of Mr. Simondson's store that night."

Well, every time those two were anywhere

near each other that morning, there was fireworks in Bob's eyes. So right after church the bomb exploded. It was the biggest church I'd ever seen, and was as long as from the corner of our bank building at Sugar Creek, clear down to the park, which is about a block away. There were more people in that one big church than live in all Sugar Creek. In fact, four times as many, 'cause there are only nine hundred eighty-seven people who live there, and that morning there were over four thousand people in church, and even more than that in Sunday school.

I say right *after* church it happened. They'd planned for us all to ride home on the L, which had a station close to Santa's apartment. he not going with us to church, but preaching in his own church in another part of Chicago. Circus was going to sing in *his* church that night.

Zipp-ety-sizzle, roar-ety-sizzle, bang-ety-sizzle, circle-ety-sizzle, our elevated train threaded its way around between the big tall buildings, dodging this way and that, following tracks, of course, with all of us sitting side by side on each side of our car, looking at each other and out the windows, listening to the noises, and looking at all kinds of people on our car and down in the streets and at hundreds of automobiles running in every direction down there. The automobiles were starting and stopping and waiting for green lights in the stop signs to tell them to start. We felt

good, 'cause again Little Jim and Circus had represented the Sugar Creek Gang, and a lot of boys our age had gone forward in the church to confess Christ.

Pretty soon we were in Santa's section of the city, which was what is called "suburban." The L came to a smooth stop, and the doors slid open. Out we went and onto the platform. And there is where the fight bomb exploded. I didn't get to hear who said what to whom, but I heard scuffling on the platform behind me. I looked just in time to see Bob's very hard fist sweep around in a fierce circle and go smashing toward Big Jim's face. At the same time Big Jim ducked, and Bob, who had swung with all his whole body behind that blow, made a complete circle, with his fist hitting nothing but some of Chicago's kinda dirty air.

It was such a vicious swing, and so hard, and Bob whirled so fast, that when Big Jim's jaw wasn't there to stop the fist, Bob lost his balance, slipped over the edge of the top step backward and then went down, with his head crashing against the side of an old iron railing. My eyes could hardly follow him, he went down so fast, down that long flight of iron steps, bumpety-bump, Bob not even trying to stop himself.

I guess I was the first one to see how he looked when he got to the bottom 'cause I was closest to the top of the stairway. I couldn't have

moved if I'd had to, 'cause I felt just like a person does when he's looking over the edge of a very high embankment and is afraid. I was as weak as a sick kitten. Maybe I'd have tumbled down myself, if my knees hadn't buckled under me and I went down kerflop on the top step.

The next thing right after that Barry was flying down to where Bob was lying very still and white and—*red!* He was bleeding terribly bad from a gash in his head.

I got to my feet and scrambled down too, along with a lot of other people, including most of the Sugar Creek Gang, although there weren't one-tenth as many people who had been on that L car as there might have been on a weekday, 'cause, as I found out later, not even a fourth of the people in Chicago go to church on Sundays. There are hundreds of thousands of children who don't go at all, their parents making them go to day school, but not to church.

Well, it seemed like I'd never seen an accident before. There at the bottom of the stairs, or rather halfway down, on a little platform where the stairway turned at a right angle before going down the rest of the way, was Bob, lying with his face right down on the end of a step, and he was pale and unconscious. There was, as I told you, a great big ugly gash on the side of his head with blood coming out of it, which means he was hemorrhaging.

Say, I wasn't only halfway down that stairs when somebody went down past me like a rocket going down, and it was Big Jim. By the time I got there, Big Jim and Barry were trying to stop the wound the way experienced Boy Scouts know how to do. But they didn't have any equipment, and it wasn't easy.

Well, that was one of the strangest experiences of my life, and it made me want to cry to see the way Big Jim looked.

Things happened pretty fast right after that. They *had* to. You know, medical doctors nearly always advise a person *not* to move anybody who has been in an automobile wreck, especially if he's been crushed in the chest or something, 'cause there might be a broken rib that might puncture a hole in a lung like a boy puncturing a balloon, or else his smashed chest wall might press against his heart and kill him. They say that in a case like that, to keep the person lying very quiet until the doctor comes, and let *him* decide what to do.

Barry, though, had been studying medicine. He saw right away there weren't any broken bones, unless maybe it would be a fractured skull which is the bony framework of a person's head, where your mind lives. In fact, *you* live there yourself, and if your house gets smashed up, *you* have to move out. I thought about that while we were on the way to the hospital, where they were

taking Bob. I thought, "What if Bob Till has to move out? Where will he go?" I knew he wasn't any dumb animal, and that he had a soul that would live forever somewhere, and that his atheist dad would be pretty much to blame if he didn't go to heaven.

In fact, while they were carrying Bob's very limp body with his new suit all messed up and spattered with blood, to Santa's car which was waiting for us at the L station, I wished every boy's parents in the world would have Bible reading at their family table and would take their children to Sunday school and church. I even wished I was President of the United States, so I could help have a law passed that would *make* every boy in America go to church, whichever one he wanted to, at least *once* a week until he was twenty-one years old. After that, maybe he'd have sense enough to go himself, and to obey God's laws.

I said that to Poetry who was sitting beside me in the taxicab while we were on our way to the hospital. "All right," he said, very seriously for him, "and I'll be vice-president. We'll declare a national emergency and start the biggest war on the devil there ever was."

I never saw such a big hospital in my life. Say! There were more sick people in that one hospital than there are *well* people in all Sugar Creek township!

After we got inside, it seemed like a very wonderful place. I don't know how I ever got to do what I did. Maybe it was because Barry knew I was going to be a doctor and arranged for me to watch what they did, which they don't generally let a boy do in a hospital, but they let me watch them give Bob Till what is called a *blood transfusion*, which means taking blood out of somebody and giving it to somebody else. They *had* to give blood to Bob Till on account of him having lost so much, and maybe he couldn't have lived without it. In fact, it looked for a while as if he might die that very afternoon.

12

WELL, BIG JIM got a chance to show Bob Till
he wasn't any coward, all right. He actually laid
down some of his life to save Bob. All the time
Bob's life was being saved, I couldn't help but
remember the time, or rather, the Battle of Bumblebee Hill in which Big Bob Till had almost
broken Big Jim's nose and the blood had come
running out for a while, until Big Jim had started
in licking the stuffin's out of Bob. Bob had hated
him ever since.

The first thing they did with Bob after they got
him into bed in that great big hospital, with nurses
busy going everywhere in a white hurry, was to
decide to give him a transfusion, and it would
have to be done *right away*. But you can't do that
as easy as it had been in my dream, when I'd
been pouring raspberry juice into somebody's veins
through a little tin funnel.

Well, this is what they did. All of us were
allowed to be in the room with Bob, who was
conscious again and lying very white and pale
on his hospital bed. We sat in chairs, or stood,

whichever we wanted to, away back from the bed like they told us to, and watched.

Big Jim stood right beside me, with his fists doubled up, only he wasn't getting ready to fight Bob but to fight *for* him.

Pretty soon an official-looking nurse came in, with a little tray in one hand, and with some glass tubes on it. She looked around a minute at all of us, and then went straight to Bob's bed, rubbed something on his finger and then pricked it with a needle.

"Wh-what's th-that for?" Dragonfly asked me, and I felt proud to think I knew what to tell him 'cause as I've told you already I'd already been studying medicine a little and was trying to learn all I could while I was little.

"That," I said with a grim face, "is to test his blood so as to find out what type it is, so she'll know what kind to give him. If you give him the wrong kind, the two won't mix right, and the blood cells will clump together and it'll *kill* him."

I guess I said the last part of it too loud, for Little Tom turned as pale as his brother Bob already was.

It took the nurse only a jiffy to do what she had to do, and she was gone.

"She's the laboratory technician," I said to the rest of the Sugar Creek Gang, trying to look very businesslike, and imagining myself to have

long, reddish-black eyebrows. Well, we kept waiting, 'cause they had in that hospital what are called "blood banks," which have blood all ready to give to people. As soon as they knew what kind you have to have, they open one of the little banks and give you some.

All the time Bob was sighing and acting very weak and faint. I can't take time now to tell you all the different things the Sugar Creek Gang said to each other or what I thought, but pretty soon I knew things weren't going to work out right. The nurse I told you about and who was what is called the "laboratory technician," found out that Bob's blood was what is called type B, and not very many people in the world have that, not more than seven out of one hundred, and the hospital didn't have any blood in their banks like that, 'cause they'd had to use it all that very morning for somebody else.

Things looked pretty bad for a while. Barry and Santa both had what is called type A, so they couldn't use *their* blood. They already knew that, and they told the doctor so.

Say, all of a sudden Big Jim's doubled-up fists doubled up still tighter and he walked over to the doctor, who had been out, and had just come in to look at us. They had been telephoning different people in the city who had type B, and couldn't find anybody who could come to the hospital. One man lived away on the other side

of the city, and it would take an hour almost for him to get there.

So Big Jim set his jaw and walked out toward that hospital cot and toward the doctor. I knew they wouldn't want any boy to be a donor, which means a giver, so I gasped. And again in my thoughts I was back in Sugar Creek, looking up toward the top of Bumblebee Hill where Bob Till and his rough, swearing gang of boys were hollering at us and calling us cowards and Sunday-school and prayer-meeting sissies. Then, with my mind's eyes, I saw Big Jim step out of the bushes where we'd been hiding, and march right up the hill toward them, and I knew he was itching to sock Big Bob on the jaw. "Fellows," he said that day, "it isn't a question of whether we're afraid to fight. There isn't a man among us that's got a drop of coward's blood in him!"

And now here we were in the hospital room, with Big Bob maybe about to die, and Big Jim was going to prove that he still didn't have a drop of coward's blood in him, and was going to offer to give his blood to save his enemy's life.

Just that second I felt Little Jim's hand push its way into one of mine, and I knew that if he could, he'd have told me something he was thinking about, which I found out afterward he was, and it was a verse from the Bible which says, "God commendeth his love toward us in that while we were yet sinners, *Christ died for us.*"

Of course doctors don't let boys be blood donors, but as I've already told you in the first of this story, Big Jim had had to have a transfusion once himself when he was littler and had lived in another town, and he happened to remember that his blood was type B.

"How old are you?" the kind doctor asked.

"Almost fifteen," Big Jim said. I noticed he was standing about half on tiptoe to make himself look tall.

Well, they had to telephone clear home to Big Jim's parents to explain it and to get their permission; and the technician had to cross-type his blood with Bob's anyway to be sure the corpuscles are what is called "compatible," which means were they *friendly* to each other and didn't *fight*. Well, they found out they didn't, and I couldn't help but remember Bumblebee Hill again.

Pretty soon it was decided. Big Jim was taken down the long hall and onto an elevator and up to the surgery room, and I was allowed to go along with Barry and him and the doctor and the technician and a nurse or two and a student nurse or two who were just learning *how* to *be* nurses.

That was a funny-looking room, with a great big chandelier up above the operating table. That table looked like my mom's ironing board only it was longer and wider and was in the center of the

119

room. They laid Big Jim down just like they were going to operate on him.

I couldn't see very well, because I had to peep through the open spaces between doctors and nurses who were standing around watching or helping. But I could see a little glass jar with a rubber bulb on top of it. There was a tube with a needle fastened to one end, and the other end was fastened to the glass jar.

Big Jim lay down flat and stretched out his arm for them to use. The next thing I knew they had a big needle stuck into one of his veins right in the crook of his arm, and then, with somebody working the rubber bulb, the glass jar began to show red in the bottom, and I knew Big Jim was giving his life's blood to save Bob Till. Once he kinda moved his head and looked over at me, and I looked at him, and I guess right that minute I never liked anybody better in all my life. I wished I could have dived in there and got hold of his other hand and squeezed it tight to let him know how I felt.

Higher and higher the little blood line crept up toward the middle of the glass jar, with the brightest red I'd ever seen, prettier than the pretty roses that grow in Mom's garden, and then I looked at Big Jim's cheeks and they weren't as red and rosy as they *had* been. Maybe if I hadn't had

Christian parents and a Sunday school teacher who believed the Bible, or if I hadn't happened to have Little Jim for a friend, I wouldn't have thought of what I did just then, but I thought for a minute of Somebody who had had *both* arms stretched out and He was hanging up high on a big, ugly wooden cross and was letting His very special blood flow out for all the sinners in the world; and whoever wants to, can believe in Him and have *everlasting life*. And do you know what? For a minute my thoughts got mixed up a little. Instead of seeing Big Jim there, I saw in my mind, Jesus Himself, who didn't have a drop of coward's blood in Him, but volunteered to die to save the whole world—and anybody in the world who will trust in the blood of Jesus to wash away his sins will be saved forever and ever.

Well, they gave Big Jim some kind of medicine right after that, and even though he was very weak for a while and a little pale, he didn't have much trouble getting over it, 'cause Big Jim was the kind of a boy that took good care of his body. He was proud of his strong body and he let God be the boss of his health and his mind too.

I hated to leave Big Jim and go down to watch them give the blood to Bob, but I thought I ought to so I could remember it to write it down for you to read, so pretty soon I was down in the hospital room with the rest of them.

It would take too long to explain it all. But in a

jiffy they had Bob's arm ready. They put a needle in the vein at the crook of his elbow, and hung up the glass jar on some kind of a standard, that was a little bit like a cross, and let the blood run down through a long tube into Bob's arm. It went down very slowly, *dripping* in, somebody told me afterward. The rest of the gang were there, so we stood in a sort of football huddle, only we weren't stooped over. We watched the whole thing, while I kept on watching Little Tom's face to see how he felt about his brother.

Pretty soon Bob's cheeks began to show a little pink, and then he looked better. He quit sighing and in just a little while he was asleep, *and his life was saved*.

Some of these things I've had to ask Barry about and some of them, my dad, and so that's how I happen to know the names for different things.

Anyway, that's the story of The Sugar Creek Gang in Chicago. Nobody in the world ever had more interesting things to see, or more fun or learned more than we did. Of course, we still had the Sunday night meeting in the church to have, and the Labor Day meeting in Santa's church, but that's too much to put into this story.

We also still had ahead of us the airplane trip back home, and on the very *next* day after we got home we had to pack up our schoolbooks and start to school.

122

Say, that reminds me! We had a new teacher that year, and like boys do sometimes when a new teacher comes, we had to find out the very first week whether she would stand for any monkey business or whether we all had to behave ourselves *all* the time. We had to try different methods, but none of them really worked, until the day Poetry tried to do what the girl in a poem did once. He let one of his dad's pet lambs follow him to school one day, only the lamb had to have a rope tied around its neck before it would follow him; and before he got it to school, it fell down into a mud puddle and its fleece wasn't as white as snow when it got there. Neither was the schoolhouse floor, after the lamb had walked around the room a while. But that was before the teacher came that morning!

Ho-hum, I suppose I'll have to rest a while before I tell you about what happened that day in a story which I'll probably name THE SUGAR CREEK GANG AT SCHOOL.